# DON ROBINSON:
# The story
# of a
# High Flier

# David Fowler

This edition published in Great Britain in 2014 by
Farthings Publishing
8 Christine House
1 Avenue Victoria
SCARBOROUGH
YO11 2QB
UK


http://www.Farthings-Publishing.com
E-mail: queries@farthings.org.uk


ISBN 978-1-291- 84747 - 5


February 2015 (s)

# DEDICATION

To Don and Jean Robinson and their family

# ACKNOWLEDGEMENTS

Grateful thanks to all the following for the use of quotes, extracts, photographs, memories and anecdotes; and in particular to Hack and Anglo Italian of Wrestling Heritage for their invaluable help with The Wrestling Years - Chapter 5.

Andrew Aldis - Bridlington Spa
Roseanne Archer
Bernard Bale
Philip Buckingham
City of Las Vegas
Dynamic Duo - Sussex
Allen Ferguson
Eileen Fowler
Frith photographs
Ian Hall and John Found
(Cricket at Scarborough)
Sarah Hutchinson-
(Bridlington Library)
Andrew Jenkinson
Wes Lawrence
Malcolm Stephenson
Merlin Entertainments Ltd
Andrew C Robinson
Saint Catherine's Hospice
Scarborough Maritime Heritage
Centre
Southwark News

The Journal, October 2006
The Scarborough News
The Times
The late Pip Waller
Wikipedia
John Woodcock
Ren Yaldren

Amusement Business magazine
Trish Atkinson
Fred Bottle
Mark Clayton
Michael Day
Brian Eastlake
John Forster
Anne Foy
Eddie Gray
Peter Hough
Hull Daily Mail
Hack & Anglo Italian

Dave Kendall
Leisure Week Magazine
Maureen Payne
Barrie Petterson
Don & Jean Robinson
Scarborough Borough Council
Viktor Sergiev

The Caterer & Hotel Keeper
magazine
The Los Angeles Times
The Theatres' Trust
The Yorkshire Post
Steve Walton
Geoff Winn
Wrestling Heritage
Yorkshire Press

# CONTENTS

Front cover graphic, and interior cartoons are by
Barrie Petterson

# OTHER BOOKS BY DAVID FOWLER:

God Bless the Prince of Wales -
www.Farthings-Publishing.com
ISBN 978-1-4092-8803-9   £11 inc UK postage

National Service, Elvis & Me!  -
www.Farthings-Publishing.com
ISBN 978-1-4092-9592-1   £13 inc UK postage

Why Should England Tremble? –
www.Farthings-Publishing.com
ISBN 978-1-4716-7748-9   £11 inc UK postage

Scarborough Snippets –
www.Farthings-Publishing.com
ISBN 978-1-291-46709-3   £11 inc UK postage

The Clock Café Story –
www.Farthings-Publishing.com
ISBN 978-1-291-48044-3   £4   inc UK postage

All are available through our website www.Farthings-Publishing.com, by e-mail: sales@farthings.org.uk
 or through www.Amazon.co.uk

# FOREWORD

Don Robinson celebrated his 80th birthday in June 2014.

He was born in Batley Carr in the West Riding of Yorkshire and when he was 10 the family moved to Scarborough in the North Riding of the County. Don left school at 14.

He excelled at sport, representing Friarage school at football and at 16 he became Yorkshire Boys' Boxing champion. He practised cricket in the nets at Scarborough Cricket Club and later went on to play professional rugby.

Just before his 18th birthday Don was called up for National Service which, he says, was his making. After initial training and an intensive course he became a PE instructor, and this earned him £1 a week extra – and a stripe. Senior Aircraftman Robinson was on his way!

Whilst in the RAF he played cricket, rugby and boxed, with the latter leading to Don appearing at London's Royal Albert Hall. On demob he returned to Scarborough to become a part time sports teacher, filling the rest of his time with yet more part time jobs. Don was always looking out for the next opportunity.

This came when he rented a small part of the beach from Scarborough Corporation and installed trampolines for use by members of the public – at a charge of course!

His first season was successful and he doubled the number of trampolines for the second. By the third, he had 12 sites throughout the country and was also selling and hiring out his trampolines.

He claims that whilst good at sport and mental arithmetic he was not academic at school but this didn't hold him back from expanding rapidly from trampolines into an amazingly diverse range of enterprises. At first, most of these were based in Scarborough but so great was his enthusiasm, vitality and verve that he expanded country wide and then later internationally, as well as into Eastern Europe when part of the Eastern bloc moved to the west.

It was Don's idea to launch Radio 270 – the very popular, so-called pirate ship in the 1960s which would operate in international waters 3 miles off the Scarborough coast.

He was responsible for the first direct charter flight from England to Las Vegas and, for this, in 1966, he was awarded the Freedom of Las Vegas City in the USA.

Much later he was made a Freeman of the City of London and later still, a Freeman of his adopted home town Scarborough.

Don Robinson became a successful wrestler under the name Dr Death. He was also a much respected wrestling promoter putting on shows, first, all over the north of England then at a 50,000 capacity stadium in India, in Sweden and elsewhere. Back home in Scarborough, he built up a vast number of leisure businesses including Flamingo Park, Scarborough Zoo and Marineland, Mr Marvel's amusement park and Water Scene outdoor swimming pool.  He then started 'It's a Knockout' at Scarborough's Open Air Theatre and lake, and expanded this event to Morecambe and Blackpool.

In 1972 he was asked to be chairman of Scarborough Football Club which had hit bad times financially. He was chairman for 10 years within which time the club made the trip to Wembley on three occasions. When he resigned and handed over, the club was solvent and in strong heart. Don had been head-hunted by the Needler family to become chairman of Hull City Football Club. He accepted to undertake a repeat, but much larger salvage operation. Again, hard graft and sound business decisions linked by common sense and his love of sport turned the club from receivership into a profitable success story for each of the 7 years he was involved.

In 1986 he was offered the prestigious role of President of Scarborough Cricket Club for a year. Most people would have jumped at the chance but Robinson demurred and only after some thought did he agree and reply that yes thank you, he was very grateful and would accept. But he had a condition. His acceptance was on condition that he could be a fully active president and not just a figurehead. His condition was accepted willingly by the committee. And fully active did Don become as he turned the club round financially, and re-established its name in cricketing circles. Unusually, he was asked, and agreed, to serve a second year as President.

He bought, refurbished and successfully ran Scarborough's Royal Opera House; and he bought the Coronia Pleasure boat and operated it for a number of seasons.

Even with his involvement in all the above he still found time in his earlier years to become a committee member of the Variety Club of Great Britain, chairman of the Zoological Association of Great Britain, to serve as a Scarborough Borough Councillor, to become a member of Lloyds of London, to be Chairman of the Malton by-pass committee and to be founder chairman of Scarborough September Carnival.

He chaired Hull Kingston Rovers Rugby team and he organised floodlit cricket at Don Valley Stadium Sheffield and at Gateshead. He owned the London, York and Paris Dungeon complexes, and, when Bulgaria became independent he was in there seeking permission for the 'Las Vegas Casino' which was agreed and built.

I have seen correspondence in which senior Ministers of the Bulgarian Government wrote to him asking for his advice on gaming and legal matters.

He became Vice President of the Stock Exchange Cricket Club, taking teams to Australia and to South Africa - where he met Nelson Mandela.

This Foreword only briefly outlines the bones of Don Robinson's achievements.

During my detailed research for this book I asked people who know him, have worked with him, or have met him in business or socially, for a brief description of Don Robinson. The calls came in: 'astute', 'colourful', 'determined', 'doesn't suffer fools gladly', 'driven', 'engaging and enthusiastic', 'entrepreneur', 'flamboyant', 'friendly', 'fun', generous; hard-grafting', 'honest', 'innovative', 'a joker', 'one of the world's great showmen', 'outgoing', 'a philanthropist', 'reliable', 'a self-made man', 'serious', 'shrewd', 'successful', unassuming'.

The only dissention to the above positivity came from what I suspect were a few diehards, and related to the time Don was Chairman of Scarborough Football club, (he made directors pay for their entry tickets when finances were in the red), President of Scarborough Cricket Club (some members apparently thought he should just get out his cheque book to bail out the club) and as a Borough Councillor. But in all three spheres Don was offering innovation, and to improve profitability and change for the better through sound business practices; there seems to have been a minority view that everything in the garden was already lovely – when it obviously wasn't - and that his efforts were unnecessary.

In the following pages I shall attempt to add flesh to the bones of this Foreword, by exploring in some detail Don Robinson's achievements in an attempt to discover what makes him tick.

My very sincere thanks to Don Robinson for all the time he has spent with me; for his patience; for dredging his memories of years long gone; and for the piles of papers and press cuttings he passed over to me from his files. Also many thanks to Don's wife Jean for allowing me to intrude on their retirement.

Don was extremely approachable and, as the book progressed I began to realise what a remarkable man he is in having achieved so much during his working life; not in one business sphere but in so many diverse fields. How he found time to achieve all he and his companies have achieved remains a mystery to me.

This book is largely a compilation of information and extracts from very many sources. There is therefore some duplication throughout the book. Also, whilst generally I have tried to keep chapters in chronological order this has not been entirely possible within chapters, with the result that there is some skipping backwards and forwards. For this I apologise.

Any errors that remain are mine alone.

I do ask that readers who spot major factual discrepancies within the book, or copyright holders who have not been acknowledged, advise me. It was not obvious from which publication some press cuttings Don handed me had come but if I am advised corrections will be made in any future edition of this book.


*David Fowler*


dgfowler@farthings.org.uk
Scarborough
July, 2014


***

# CHAPTER ONE

## 1934–1962 The early years

Don Robinson was born on 27th June 1934 and lived in the family home at Taylor Street, Batley Carr in West Yorkshire. Batley Carr is a district between Dewsbury and Batley.

The population then was about 3,740 and originally Batley Carr housed the workers from the nearby mills. As the settlement expanded with the growth of textiles there was a necessity for its own railway station - Staincliffe and Batley Carr railway station. The red brick station master's house still stands but is now a private residence.

However, Batley Carr has since dwindled in size and now only has a post office, a few shops, remaining houses, a night club and some working men's clubs.

Don's father was called Joe and was a storeman. His mother was May, née Wray. Don had one older stepbrother called Basil who died some years ago.

In 1938, before World War II and when Don was 4 the family moved to Green Hammerton to live with his grandmother. Don attended Green Hammerton Infants school but when he moved up to the Juniors the nearest school was at Whixley, about a mile away.

There was a school bus – even in those days - but if Don and his friends missed the bus they would walk home across the fields and halve the distance.

In 1944 when he was 10 years old the family moved to Dean Road in Scarborough and he attended Friarage Junior school for a year before moving up to the senior school.

Don loved that school. He played football for the school team and, in the summer and after school would practice cricket in the nets at Scarborough Cricket Club in North Marine Road. He says,

'I wasn't too bright at school. My spelling was poor but I was good at mental arithmetic and sport and whilst I would have liked to go to University it wasn't to be. University can be useful for the professions but if a young person isn't that way inclined they are surely better training on the job and earning a wage at the same time. I do worry about young people these days that seem to get the impression that if they don't go to University they have failed in life. That's absolute rubbish. Look at me. I am nearly 80 and I left school at 14 which was not unusual in those days. I was determined to enjoy my life and to cram as much into it as I possibly could. I was also determined to make a success of it although that intention was probably triggered by National Service. I looked out for opportunities along the way and as they arose I grasped them as I knew that if I didn't, someone else would.'

Don may have been a late developer academically but he obviously had well above average intelligence to go on to achieve so much during his lifetime.

His first employment after leaving school was as a trainee salesman in the 'boys' private school clothing department' at Scarborough's Marshall and Snelgrove – then probably the most upmarket store in the town. He was also part time lift boy for the store when the regular lift man was away for which he had to wear 'a little brown suit and a little brown pillbox hat'.

Don says, 'They changed my outlook all those well-to-do customers. I suppose part of it was to do with class-consciousness. Whatever, it made me want to be a success.'

Always keen on sport, Don became Yorkshire Boy's Boxing champion at 16 then, just before his 18th birthday in 1953 he was called up for National Service in the RAF.

DON ROBINSON
YORKSHIRE BOYS
CHAMPION 1950

He agreed to extend his service to 3 years from the normal 2 and after initial training he underwent a gruelling selection process to become a PE instructor.

He recalls, 'There were 16 applicants and only 6 positions. The pass mark was 60% and I scraped in at number 6 with a score of 60.01%.'

This success earned him £1 a week extra – and a stripe. Senior Aircraftman Robinson was on his way!

Whilst in the RAF Don played cricket and rugby for the Command teams. He says he was 'mad on rugby both to watch and play' and he played for the RAF when he passed out as a PE instructor and was posted to RAF Rufforth. From Rufforth he was also able to get back home at the weekends where he would play cricket for Scarborough Reserves.

His earlier aptitude for boxing led to him boxing for the RAF as a light welterweight and in a match RAF v the Amateur Boxing Association he became Light Welterweight champion - in London's Royal Albert Hall. This was at a time, Don says, 'when I was barely twenty and I had never ever been to London, so not visited, let alone performed in the Royal Albert Hall with its capacity of over 5000 people!'

Maybe that was when the entertainment bug really bit him.

On demob, and by now aged just 21, he returned to Scarborough, and with his RAF PE qualifications and experience he quickly moved on and got a part-time job as a PE instructor at the then Scarborough Technical College which was moving to a new site in Scarborough on Scalby Road.

After 4 years there, during which time he had also played professional Rugby for Hull Kingston Rovers, (yet also found time to run various part-time businesses such as driving instructor, fish and chip shop proprietor, café proprietor, perfume manufacturer ('Black Narcissus'?) and wet fish stall proprietor at Wallis's Cayton Bay Holiday Camp), the College Principal called Don in and said he was impressed by his verve, enthusiasm and 'people skills' which he felt, 'encouraged the youngsters to give of their best'.

As a result he offered Don a full-time role as PE teacher.

But despite the offer of a good salaried position and pensionable employment, Don thought long and hard before turning the offer down. He had seen the enthusiasm with which the students had taken to the college's new trampolines.

Don says, 'National Service was the best thing that ever happened to me. I learned a lot about discipline with which I agreed and with my interest in sport I was very fit and intended making a success of my life.

Don remembers, 'I got into business if a funny way. After demob from the RAF I returned to Scarborough and became a part-time PE Teacher at Scarborough Technical College. It was moving to a new building on a site on Scalby Road just beyond the hospital where it would eventually become known as the Yorkshire Coast College. There was a new gymnasium to equip and the college was importing large trampolines from the USA at £240 each plus carriage. When they arrived the kids loved them and I had this idea that they would be great to use on the beach for holidaymakers. But £240 each plus carriage was well beyond my means in those days so I designed trampolines to my own specifications, then approached local firms who made 6 for me  for a total of £180 – only £30 each. I got permission from the Corporation and I ran them on Scarborough beach and they took off like wildfire. I called them 'Jumping Jiminies'.

'I did well in my first season so I got another 6 for the following year. At the end of that season I checked my profits, then checked them again, then for the 3rd year I bought extra trampolines and expanded so that for that year I had a further 12 sites all over the country. Not only did I have people run these trampolines on the beaches for me but I also hired out and sold my design of trampoline.

'I learned a lot about business from this venture – management, checking tills, tickets, staffing, budgets and so on. The impetus I got from running my trampolines was also the start of a learning curve which taught me about the intricacies of successful business, book keeping, balance sheets, the stock market, shares and so on.'

'I originally ran the business in my own name but then incorporated my first company, Beach Management Ltd. In 1962 I sold the sites in other parts of the country to their operators but continued the Scarborough site for some time.

During this period Don had a regular girlfriend. They were similar ages with Jean Margaret Towell having been born just weeks before Don.

They had met, become friends, courted and fallen in love and they married at St Columba's Church on the corner of Dean Road and Columbus Ravine, Scarborough, in 1955.

Now, nearly 60 years, two sons and their families, numerous business start-ups, acquisitions and sales later, they remain happily married.

# CHAPTER 2

## 1963 – The Flamingo Park Years

Flamingoland, based at Kirby Misperton between Malton and Pickering in North Yorkshire, was originally opened as the Yorkshire Zoological Gardens in 1959 on a site only 9 acres in area.

Now, fifty five years later and much extended, it attracts about 1.8 million visitors a year and is the 12th most visited theme park in Europe.

The attraction was born from an old, small and bankrupt country club which was bought by a Scarborough resident, an entrepreneur in the cinema and theatre industry called Edwin Pentland Hick. Pentland Hick as he preferred to be called, had grand ideas for the park; a vision which he had nurtured since military service during World War II. Hick has been described as both an eccentric and a visionary by his critics and friends. He couldn't afford to buy animals in the early days so hired them until receipts allowed him to buy his own.

Don Robinson joined him and they formed the company Flamingo Park Ltd. They wanted to have a zoo and dolphins in their park. Dolphins were not found in captivity in the UK at that time.

In 1963 the purchase of land increased the size of the park to 25 acres. They organized expeditions to many locations around the world to obtain bottlenose dolphins and sperm whales, including to the Indian Ocean and off the coast of Greenland. They were commended for their treatment of the animals, which were fed well and kept in expansive enclosures.

Steve Walton was dolphin trainer from the early days and over the intervening years he has kept in touch with Don. In 2014 Don says,

'Steve was wonderful with the dolphins and I held him in very high regard and still do. He was a natural and I still see him occasionally and he's done very well for himself, now being dolphin consultant for two large international firms.'

In turn, Steve Walton said recently about Don:

'I have known Don well for well over 40 years and first met him in the days of Zoo & Marineland when I was appointed Dolphin trainer.

He was a great boss and we were like one big happy family. We all worked together in our different roles and Zoo & Marineland was only converted into Mr Marvels because of the climate changing against animals being kept in captivity. Don was a great man to work for and had a great sense of jollity and fun. Since our paths separated. we have always kept in touch. I specialised in Dolphins and everything to do with them and became a consultant to firms all over the world.'

*

A colony of pink flamingos was among the first species to be housed on the site and, being one of the most popular group of birds in the zoo, the flamingos became an attraction and talking point for the entire park, hence the final choice of name for the park.

Even though the enterprise has changed hands a number of times since then, the descendants of the original flamingos are still resident in the zoo today and the flamingo colony at the park remains the largest in the country.

Throughout the 1960s a small fun fair was opened on the site which steadily gained momentum and brought more and more visitors to the site.

Don sold his shareholding in 1964 and the same year the company was floated on the London Stock Exchange as Associated Pleasure Parks Limited. The site was renamed Flamingo Park Zoo on Monday 12 July 1968.

The ICI pension Fund became a large shareholder and the ownership of the business began to change with the steady growth of the park, eventually being sold in full to Scotia Leisure Ltd, a company which dealt mainly with bingo halls, a casino and Bailey's Hotel in London, together with package holidays. Don Robinson was a shareholder in Scotia Leisure and its associate company, Scotia Pleasure Parks Ltd which also owned Cleethorpes Winter Gardens, Dudley Zoo and Cricket St Thomas Zoo. The main directors were Robin Buchanan, Don Robinson, David Cook (the latter two both based in Scarborough) and Jim Jackson who was based in Cleethorpes. Around this time, George Jackson (no relative of Jim), a recently retired Barclays Bank Manager from Scarborough, joined the company in the role of finance officer.

*

Don Robinson has a life-long reputation as a practical joker and whilst he does not claim credit for the following story, he was obviously involved. And it is obvious that it was not 'all work and no play', as it is claimed that Flamingo Park Zoo created the world's 3rd best ever April Fool's Day hoax of all time, on 1st April 1972.

## 'The body of Nessie found - 1st April 1972

On the morning of Friday March 31st, 1972, an eight-member team of scientists from Yorkshire's Flamingo Park Zoo was having breakfast in the dining room of the Foyers House hotel, on the shore of Loch Ness. They were there on a joint mission with the Loch Ness Phenomena Bureau to prove the existence of a monster in the loch. They had developed a new form of 'hormone sex bait' that they hoped would lure Nessie out of the depths.

As they dug into their bacon and eggs, the manager of the hotel approached them. Someone had just called, she said, to report seeing a 'large hump' floating in the loch near the hotel. Intrigued, the team put down their knives and forks and walked outside. Sure enough, a large, dark object was bobbing up and down in the waves about 300 yards offshore.

Terence O'Brien, the leader of the team, immediately swung into action. He directed the team into their boat, and they headed out to investigate. Twenty minutes later, at around 9 am, they returned, dragging behind them a bizarre object. It appeared to be the dead body of the Loch Ness Monster.

Within hours, news of the discovery had reached the rest of the world. Television news anchors solemnly informed their audiences that the Loch Ness Monster had been found, but was dead. Reporters rushed to the loch to get more details.

Local residents confirmed that something weird had been dragged out of the water. Robert MacKenzie, a 23-year-old Inverness musician, said, 'I touched it and put my hand in its mouth. It's real, all right. I thought it looked half-bear and half-seal. It was green in colour with a horrific head like a bear with flat ears. I was shocked.'

Other witnesses told reporters the creature had been between 12 and 18 feet in length and must have weighed up to 1½ tons. They said it had a green body without scales and was like a cross between a walrus and a seal.

Eventually reporters contacted Don Robinson, Director of the Flamingo Park Zoo, who said, 'I've always been sceptical about the Loch Ness Monster, but this is definitely a monster, no doubt about that. From the reports I've had, no one has ever seen anything like it before... a fishy, scaly body with a massive head and big protruding teeth.'

*Scene from the 1969 United Artists' thriller 'The Private Life of Sherlock Holmes'*

The next morning, April 1st, the discovery made front-page headlines around the world. The British press dubbed the creature 'Son of Nessie.'

Meanwhile, the creature itself was no longer at the Loch. After dragging the carcass back to the shore, the scientists from the Flamingo Park Zoo had sent a telegram to their boss, Don Robinson, and had then quickly loaded the body into their truck and taken off, intending to transport the monster back to the Scarborough zoo for study.

The police officers, not quite sure what to do next, radioed back to the station for advice. They were told to take the monster to the nearest town, Dunfermline, where it would be examined by Scottish scientists.

Mrs Margrete Good, manager of the hotel, later told the press, 'The zoologists were thrilled to bits.'

# 'Monster' Hauled Out of Loch Ness

*April 1, 1972 headline in the Los Angeles Times*

But when the local Inverness police heard that the scientists had hightailed it with the Loch Ness Monster, they were infuriated. These were English scientists, after all, removing Scotland's most famous lake monster — upon which depended a vast, lucrative tourist trade.

Immediately the police radioed their colleagues in the Fifeshire County police department, explained the situation, and asked them to chase the fleeing truck and apprehend the monster-nappers.

*'Never mind saying they're gaining on us - I thought you said this thing was dead?!*

They cited a 1933 Act of Parliament that prohibited the removal of 'unidentified creatures' from Loch Ness. Bells clanging, the police cars sped off. They soon caught up with the team of scientists. The frightened zoologists readily cooperated with the police, pulling over to the side of the road, and then opening the back of the truck to show the officers what they were carrying. Sure enough, according to the subsequent police report, lying inside the truck was a large 'green and scaly' creature.

In Dunfermline, the police searched around for an appropriate scientist to examine the creature, and eventually persuaded Michael Rushton, general curator of the Edinburgh Zoo, to come up and look at it.

When Rushton arrived, he walked slowly around the carcass a few times, poked it once or twice, and then announced his verdict. It was indeed a strange creature, but it was no lake monster. Instead, it was a bull elephant seal, whose natural home was the South Atlantic Ocean, thousands of miles away from Scotland. Furthermore, the body showed signs of having been frozen for an extended period of time.

Rushton told the press, 'It is a typical member of its species. It's about 3 to 4 years old. I have never known them to come near Great Britain. Their natural habitat is the South Atlantic, Falkland Islands or South Georgia. I don't know how long it's been kept in a deep freeze but this has obviously been done by some human hand.'

How a bull elephant seal came to be floating in Loch Ness remained a mystery until the next day, when a hoaxer stepped forward to confess. John Shields, the Flamingo Park Zoo's education officer, admitted it was his doing.

Shields explained that an expedition to the Falkland Islands had recently brought the seal back to the UK. It had lived briefly at Dudley Zoo, but died soon after arrival. When he learned of this, Shields realized it offered an opportunity to carry out a prank on his colleagues, who he knew were going up to Loch Ness to search for the monster.

Shields gained possession of the elephant seal, shaved off its whiskers, padded its cheeks with stones, and kept it frozen for a week. Then he dumped it in the Loch and tipped off the hotel to make sure his colleagues found it. He timed the prank so that news of the discovery of the Loch Ness Monster would make headlines on April 1st — April Fool's Day, which happened to also be his 23rd birthday.

Shields admitted the joke got out of hand when his colleagues decided to remove the dead animal from Loch Ness and were chased by the police.

He also noted that the creature wasn't quite as impressive as initial press reports had claimed. It was only nine feet long and weighed 350 pounds. Still, it had been a very strange thing to find floating in the Loch.

Police Superintendent Inas McKay of Inverness gave the press the final, official verdict on the incident: 'It's just an April Fool's Day joke.'

*The "monster" on display at the Flamingo Park Zoo*

Having determined that the dead animal was not the Loch Ness Monster, the police had no further interest in it. So they returned the carcass to the team from Flamingo Park Zoo. The team took the seal back to the zoo, where they put it back on ice and displayed it to crowds for a few days before properly disposing of it.

But this wasn't quite the end of the story which appeared as headlines in Sunday papers throughout the world.

Don Robinson held a Christmas Press Lunch on 6th December 1973 at Kirby Misperton Hall. The menu card cover is reproduced with the cartoon and wording at the foot obviously intended as a dig at the press members who attended the lunch.

Also reproduced is a letter, supposedly from Ted Heath at 10 Downing Street who was then Prime Minister, and a telegram (below) from Harold Wilson. Don is convinced they are all genuine – but forty one years later other acquaintances who attended the lunch are not so sure!

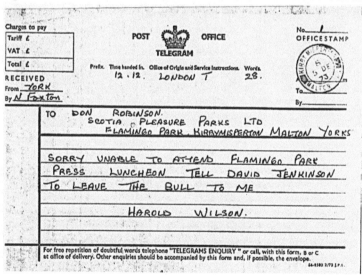

*The telegram received from 'Harold Wilson', leader of the Opposition. The David Jenkinson it refers to was a well-known Scarborough Councillor and businessman at the time of the lunch.*

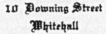

10 Downing Street
Whitehall

The Prime Minister thanks
Mr. Don Robinson for his kind
invitation to a Christmas Press
Luncheon at the Flamingo Park
Zoo on Thursday 6 December but
much regrets that, owing to other
engagements, he is unable to
accept.

29 November 1973

*The letter from 'The Prime Minister, 10 Downing Street Whitehall'*
*apologising that PM Ted Heath could not attend.*

*Above: The press lunch menu depicting the Loch Ness Monster. We can confirm that the man hanging from the YTV helicopter was Don Robinson!*

Very recently I met Brian Eastlake who at the time of the Loch Ness Monster hoax, had been a telephone engineer in the Pickering and Kirby Misperton areas. He had been maintaining the Flamingo Park lines within the park and whilst he noticed a lot of coming and going and much activity, it was only later he realised that the 'Monster' had achieved world-wide press coverage on April 1st. "And I was there at Flamingo Park at the time but didn't realise what was happening!" he says.

\*

In 1974, Don moved on and a major zoo revamp took place under David Cook and Kevin Taylor, the recently recruited Marketing Director. Howell Jones Sneider Weaver, a London advertising agency with a base in Yorkshire, was appointed and, using Disney as inspiration, Flamingo Park was renamed Flamingoland. More emphasis was placed on the 'day out' experience, with fairground rides, a haunted castle, model railway and a jungle cruise raft ride on the lake; all this using the animals in the zoo as the core. Flamingoland also had a static caravan, mobile home, and touring caravan site - as well as Kirby Misperton Hall, the stately home at the centre of the estate, which had first attracted Hick to the area. The hall was used as a popular venue for local hunt balls and a regular Saturday evening Dinner Dance and Cabaret called The Continental.

Despite a more professional marketing approach led by Taylor, which saw regular guest appearances by celebrities and stars of the day (including the racehorse Red Rum!), Flamingo Land lost money and it was thought that it could close and the animals would have to be dispersed to other zoos.

However one of the directors of Scotia Leisure was called Robert Gibb and he had been in charge of the company's bingo division until it was sold to Coral. Gibb saw an opportunity and decided to offer to buy the park from the company in 1978, shortly before Scotia Leisure collapsed due to an embezzlement scandal that also left Pentland Hick broke.

Hick had long since had had nothing to do with Flamingoland, moving into theatre and television scriptwriting and becoming an author. Meanwhile, Robert Gibb set up his own board of directors for the park and formed Flamingo Land Ltd with Kevin Taylor as Director & general manager with day to running responsibility and Trevor Pullen in charge of the catering. Wholesale redundancies ensued amongst the staff, apart from the animal keepers, as a more or less permanent staff had been kept on throughout the winter periods, leeching any profit that might have been made in the summers. Most of the redundant staff was then re-engaged on seasonal contracts.

*Above: The Pinfari Zyklon Coaster*

Gibb, with Taylor and Pullen, developed the complex so that it was more suited to be a nationwide instead of a local tourist attraction. This included developing the growth of the amusement rides and the uniqueness of the animals in the zoo. Initially the restructuring was successful and some innovative and creative management saw the park make a profit after just one year, the first time it had done so for over a decade. Kevin Taylor was head-hunted by the then under construction Thorpe Park in Surrey at the end of 1978. Flamingo Land's recovery was a slow process, but eventually a successful one. The year 1991 (whilst the park was still under Robert Gibb's management) was one of the most productive in the park's history; it was in this year that the famous rides Bullet and Thunder Mountain were constructed.

Robert Gibb tragically died in a car accident in 1995; Pullen also died. Gibb's son Gordon Gibb, who was only 18 at the time, took control of the park with the rest of the family, later becoming the chief executive of Flamingo Land Ltd.

Flamingo Land, claimed to be the largest animal holder of its kind in Europe, housed over 1,000 animals, exotic birds, rare fish, mammals and reptiles. The animals include camels, zebras, guanaco, hippopotamuses, giraffes, meerkats, baboons, chimpanzees, lions, rhinoceroses, tigers, sea lions, parrots, and peacocks – as well, of course as flamingos.

The park's emphasis was on their collection of African animals, housed in the Lost Kingdom and African Plains sections of the park. The water ride (the Lost River Ride) was designed to give a safari experience, and meanders through Savannah-style grasslands with giraffes, ostriches, zebras, hippos and rhinos. The 'Forgotten City Lion Reserve' is also located in the middle of the ride.

The park has a large holiday village with static caravans and log cabins. In the holiday village there are leisure facilities including a leisure centre, a swimming pool and a café.

On the outskirts of the park lies a nine-hole golf course. Also adjacent to the park runs Costa Beck, a stream locally noted for crystal clear water and fly fishing is available here free to those staying in the holiday village. Trout, dace, grayling, salmon, and pike can all be found in Costa Beck.

Also in the holiday village is the American Bar, an entertainments venue which is exclusive for caravan owners and people staying on site overnight. It is a venue capable of holding over 1000 people and boasts a large stage and resident shows as well as light entertainment performed by visiting cabaret acts.

Flamingo land continues to go from strength to strength and is now open for the 2014 season.

# CHAPTER 3

## 1964 – The Radio 270 years
## Little Richard

In 1964 Ellambar Investments Limited was incorporated, as, earlier in the 1960s Don Robinson had started to think about, then to plan, an offshore commercial radio station which would be funded by advertising and provide a service both to the advertisers and the likely large number of listeners who had only two BBC stations in the UK to listen to at that time. Neither of these played much of the popular or 'pop' music preferred by the younger generation.

Don planned to call it Radio Yorkshire.

Radio Caroline started transmissions on Easter Sunday 1964 and this spurred Don on.

In 1965 Robinson, then aged 31, gathered a group of Yorkshire businessmen and formed a consortium to establish an offshore radio station to broadcast to the North East coast from a location 3 miles off Scarborough in international waters. Don Robinson, by then an entertainments promoter, began the venture with Bill Pashby (a fishing boat skipper), Roland Hill (a poultry farmer) and Leonard Dale (Chairman of Dale Electric at Gristhorpe near Scarborough). These four recruited Wilf Proudfoot, owner of a small chain of local supermarkets and a former Conservative MP. The venture was incorporated within a public company named Ellambar Investments Ltd.

Pirate radio is a bit of a misnomer as the company was properly constituted and English law at that time merely prevented a commercial radio station operating from within the country or within the 3 mile international maritime boundary.

In late 1965, Proudfoot addressed a public meeting at a Scarborough hotel in which he invited the public to subscribe for shares in the business. He indicated that the venture was high risk and that nobody should expect a commercial return on the money they put in. Around sixty people did subscribe with the largest single shareholding being held by Proudfoot himself. Leonard Dale became Chairman of the company while Proudfoot became its managing director.

Don Robinson and Bill Pashby both initially occupied prominent roles in what soon became known as Radio

270. Robinson prepared the first programme plan for the station which adopted a mixture of light music and lifestyle material. It was intended to provide an 'up-market' offering which would compete directly with the BBC's Light Programme. Pashby was the station's first 'Maritime Director' and it was he that picked out a suitable vessel for use as a broadcasting platform and supervised its fitting out.

However, the business side of the operation fell increasingly under the control of Wilf Proudfoot. The station's management was run from an office in Scalby road, Scarborough, which also happened to be the headquarters of the Proudfoot supermarket business and also Proudfoot's own home. The station's office manager was Maggie Lucas, a long standing associate of Proudfoot who had acted as his secretary when he had been the Member of Parliament for Cleveland from 1959 to 1964.

Proudfoot became uncomfortable with the planned programming and he engaged the services of Noel Miller as Programme Director. Miller had previous experience of commercial radio in Australia and he adopted a simple style of programming based on a Top 40 format.

A planned opening date of 1 April 1966 had to be abandoned when the station's vessel, by then renamed Ocean 7, shed its radio mast. However, the station finally opened in June, broadcasting on 269 metres in the medium wave. This wavelength was used by some existing radio stations in southern and Eastern Europe but these were too far away for Radio 270 to cause them any trouble. The initial results were highly successful. The station's broadcasts could be received over a large tract of eastern England from Newcastle in the north to Nottingham in the south, containing as many as 15 million people. It even gained some listeners in the Netherlands. Its continuous pop music format attracted a regular audience which various estimates placed between 1.5 and 4 million for which the BBC did not then cater.

The station charged a basic £30 for a 30 second advertising spot. It was very successful in attracting advertising for local businesses and events in the North Yorkshire area. Even Scarborough Borough Council paid for twelve 15 second adverts to announce events in the town's Festival of Norway. However, big-ticket advertising for national businesses proved elusive. The largest single paying advertiser was the Worldwide Church of God which purchased a nightly 30 minute slot for a fee of around £300 per week. This covered most of Radio 270's payroll. The nightly 'God slot' contained the preaching of evangelist Garner Ted Armstrong.

The second largest advertiser was the Proudfoot supermarket group. This created a somewhat complex financial situation in which there were two-way transfer charges between Radio 270 and Wilf Proudfoot for reciprocal services rendered.

\*

In 1965, the promoters of Radio 270 had identified a Dutch built fishing lugger named Oceaan VII as being suitable for their purposes. This was acquired for £2,500.

The Oceaan VII was built in the Netherlands in 1939 and had spent most of its life operating out of the Belgian port of Antwerp. During World War II it had been commandeered by the German occupation forces. It was approximately 118 feet long and 160 tonnes in displacement. The vessel was refitted in the east coast port of Grimsby before being brought to Scarborough where it was renamed Ocean 7. The refit involved the addition of 20 tonnes of permanent ballast in the hull in order to give extra stability. The vessel was fitted with a 150 feet high radio mast and a 10 kW RCA transmitter. The vessel's main engine was a four cylinder 240 hp diesel. Two newly installed 50 kva Dale Marine generators supplied all electricity needed for operational purposes.

There were two studios on board, one for presenting programmes and one for news. Accommodation for crew and broadcasting staff was both confined and spartan. Living quarters consisted of a bunk room with a dining table in the middle. Food was provided from a communal galley.

The entire cost of acquiring and fitting out the vessel was £75,000. The crewing was initially planned to be on a one month rotation basis. The ship's entire eight man crew including the captain were switched every month. Broadcasting staff, including disc jockeys, initially worked on a two week rotation basis.

The Ocean 7 was among the smallest of the pirate radio ships at that time. By way of comparison, Radio London broadcast from the 650 tonne MV Galaxy positioned in the Thames estuary. Ocean 7's initial location off Scarborough allowed its signal to be widely received over the North of England but left the vessel totally exposed to storms in the North Sea.

Ocean 7 was registered in Honduras in the name of Radio 270's Programme Director Noel Miller (an Australian national). This effectively placed the vessel beyond the reach of the British authorities. Most pirate radio ships were kept supplied from shore by tender. However Ocean 7's small size allowed it to periodically enter Bridlington and Scarborough harbours for re-supply purposes. The visits to harbour were usually carried out in the early hours of the morning in order to avoid disruption to broadcasting and to minimise the chances of intervention by the authorities.

Although Radio 270 quickly established itself as a successful local radio station, its affairs soon became complicated. Various factors contributed to this.

Ocean 7 was very small for the purpose to which it was being put. The cramped living accommodation and lack of privacy on board soon caused tensions among the personnel. It proved difficult to maintain the vessel in position off Scarborough as the winter storms came. In November 1966 one storm was so severe that waves were breaking over the vessel's deck and water entered the living quarters and studio. The station carried on broadcasting through the early part of the storm although the presenters were obviously in fear for their lives. Listeners on-shore (including 270 staff member Paul Burnett) were horrified by what was happening. In the aftermath of the storm, the station went off the air for 8 days while repairs were carried out.

Some of the shareholders became concerned about the degree to which Radio 270's business was being integrated within that of Wilf Proudfoot. Issues relating to the latter's management style were raised.

Conditions of employment and rates of pay were not generous. Consequently, there were a series of disputes with personnel and staff turnover rates became high. Matters came to a head after the November storm when Proudfoot was approached by three disc jockeys (including 19 year old Andy Kirk) with a demand that Ocean 7 should move its station to a more sheltered location in Bridlington Bay or put into harbour whenever bad weather threatened. Kirk had previously conveyed his concerns about safety to the local press. Proudfoot summarily dismissed all three of the DJs.

A number of the shareholders now became restless and two attempts were made to oust Proudfoot from his post of managing director. Both of these attempts failed. Bill Pashby resigned as Maritime Director and said he was "...fed up with the continuous sackings of the crew". Proudfoot eventually responded to these concerns by moving Ocean 7's position to Bridlington Bay while moving to a one week staff rotation for most on-board personnel. The move to Bridlington Bay gave more settled conditions but it worsened reception of Radio 270's signal across large parts of its audience catchment area.

The living conditions on the Radio 270 ship were not pleasant. It was extremely cramped. To add to their discomfort, some of the DJs were prone to sea-sickness. Paul Burnett even endured the ultimate indignity of throwing up live on air - while reading a commercial for Proudfoot bacon! There was a high turnover of disc-jockeys and a certain amount of technical trouble, both of which upset the investors. On a couple of occasions Wilf Proudfoot had to contend with stormy shareholders meetings. However he survived their attempts to oust him.

By early 1967, Radio 270's affairs seemed to be stabilising and it was reported that the station was breaking-even financially.

The pirate radio stations attracted opposition from within the British political establishment. It was claimed that their broadcasts interfered with emergency service communications, and this led to enactment of the Marine Offences Broadcasting Act of 1967, which took effect at midnight on 14 August of that year. This Act prohibited the management, funding, support or supply of pirate radio ships from the British mainland.

The pirate stations campaigned against the Act during the early months of 1967. Radio 270 was prominent in this campaign and its contributions to the campaign took on an overtly political dimension. A group of Conservative MPs and activists became involved with Radio 270. These included the MP for Beverley, Patrick Wall. The station gave airtime to a number of political causes including a broadcast by Wall in which he advocated British recognition of the white minority UDI regime in Rhodesia. Radio 270 broadcast advertisements supporting Conservative party candidates in the Scarborough municipal elections of 1967. Harvey Proctor, then Chairman of the University of York Conservative Society, made regular half hour current affairs broadcasts. Proctor went on to have a controversial career as a Conservative MP and prominent member of the Conservative Monday Club.

This appeared to harden the Labour government's resolve to deal with the pirates. Postmaster-General Edward Short stated about Radio 270 that, 'It is the first time in peacetime that this country has been subjected to a stream of misleading propaganda from outside our territorial waters and I do not think this is a matter for joking'.

As 14 August approached, it was initially suggested that Radio 270 could continue broadcasting were Ocean 7 to be supplied from the Netherlands and the station's management being shifted to that country. However, it was soon realised that this was not a viable option. DJ Vince 'Rusty' Allen closed the station at one minute to midnight on 14 August 1967, its broadcasting career being brought to an end in 1967 as a result of the Marine Broadcasting Offences Act.

On 15 August Ocean 7 sailed up the coast to Whitby. It was laid up there whilst a buyer was sought. It was advertised for sale via Tuckley and Co, a local estate agent with a reputation for amusing property adverts. Various enquiries were received from prospective buyers including one from the operators of Radio Caroline, whose own ships had been seized by creditors. However, none of these enquiries resulted in a sale. The transmitter and other broadcasting equipment from Radio 270 were placed in storage and in 1970 found their way to the Dutch-based pirate Capital Radio (which had no connection to the later British radio station of the same name). Ocean 7 was scrapped in 1969.

The proceeds from the disposal of the vessel and its equipment raised a total of around £12,500. By the time creditors had been paid off there was no cash available to allow a significant return of capital to the Radio 270 shareholders. As far as is known, none of the shareholders ever achieved a direct financial return on their investment.

Wilf Proudfoot stood as the Conservative candidate in the marginal West Yorkshire constituency of Brighouse and Spenborough, where he ousted the sitting Labour MP Colin Jackson by a majority of only 59 votes. The closure of the pirate radio stations is believed to have been a key issue in a number of marginal seats. Proudfoot himself lost his seat in the February 1974 general election. Thereafter he spent some time in the USA where he trained as a hypnotist in Los Angeles. He later established the Proudfoot School of Clinical Hypnotism and Psychotherapy based in Scarborough.

Don Robinson continued his career as an events promoter and entrepreneur. He is credited with having saved Hull City football club ('The Tigers') from extinction in 1982 when he bought the club out of receivership. As club Chairman from 1982 to 1989 he presided over a revival in the club's financial and football fortunes that saw it enjoy a series of league promotions. The newly promoted Hull City narrowly retained its Premier League status in the 2008/09 football season.

Many former Radio 270 staff, such as Roger Gale, Paul Burnett, Philip Hayton and Mark Wesley went on to enjoy distinguished careers in mainstream broadcasting. The station's office manager, Maggie Lucas, went on to become secretary to the Chairman of the Australian Broadcasting Commission. Although Radio 270's life was brief, it had a significant impact on North East England and many tributes were paid to it on the 40th anniversary of its closure.

DJ Paul Burnett recalls, 'Although a dynamic leader, Wilf Proudfoot was possibly an odd choice to run a Top 40 radio station. It soon became apparent that he did not hold the skills of a disc-jockey in particularly high regard. I remember when we weren't presenting shows, Wilf expected us to be doing odd jobs on the ship - chipping rust, painting, etc. I remember being with him and he was saying things like, 'anyone can be a DJ'. There was a young spotty lad there, probably about 17, delivering groceries. Proudfoot turned to him and said 'Ee lad, do you fancy being a disc-jockey?' The boy rather hesitantly said that he did, so Proudfoot hired him and sent him out to the ship - to do the Breakfast Show! He was only there a week. He went off on leave at the end of his first stint and we never saw him again.'

As well as carrying out routine maintenance jobs on the ship, the DJs were expected to help sell airtime during their shore-leave. Some enjoyed this - but many did not! Although not all the staff appreciated Proudfoot, Radio 270 was a well-run operation. During its short life – it was on air for less than 15 months - the station earned some £100,000 in advertising revenue, paid its initial start-up bill and broke even on its running costs. This was a major achievement and much of the credit must go to its Managing Director, Wilf Proudfoot.

Radio 270 gave free air-time to various charities. Oxfam, the Salvation Army and the Royal National Lifeboat Institute were all promoted on the station. In addition £500 was raised for the Wireless for the Blind Fund by selling car stickers at one (old) penny each. There was also extensive advertising, of course, for Proudfoot Supermarkets with the DJs often mentioning that they were shops 'where the doors open by themselves' - this being something of a novelty in the sixties.

Throughout its existence Radio 270 campaigned heavily for the introduction of licenced commercial radio as the introduction of the Marine Offences Bill made its way through Parliament. Sadly their efforts were in vain. The Act became law at midnight on 14th August 1967 and Radio 270 closed down.

Wilf Proudfoot died on 19th July 2013, leaving his wife Peggy, to whom he was married for 63 years, sons Mark and Ian, the joint managing directors of the Proudfoot supermarket company, a daughter Lyn and five grandchildren. He was 91.

*

A report appeared in 2003 from The Dynamic Duo in Derbyshire:

'Some of television's biggest stars are to descend on the North Yorkshire coast when shooting begins for a new film in Scarborough.

Making Waves, based on the town's famous pirate radio ship 270, will start filming in the spring of 2004. Starring well-known actors Michael Gambon, Richard E Grant and Johnny Vegas, as well as TV presenter Angus Deayton, the film enhances the region's growing tradition for movie blockbusters.

Making Waves follows the likes of Little Voice, starring Michael Caine, the yet to be released Miranda and the appearance of Oscar winning actress Gwyneth Paltrow in Possession, which was filmed in Whitby.

It also follows hot on the heels of the first Harry Potter movie, which was partly filmed on the North Yorkshire Moors.

Councillor David Jeffels, Scarborough Borough Council's cabinet member for tourism and leisure, said: "It is excellent that our East Coast is once again going to provide the backdrop for a film.

Movies like this, and television series like Heartbeat, get this beautiful part of the country priceless exposure.

We pride ourselves on being a film-friendly location and always do what we can to accommodate film crews.

The pirate radio station is part of Scarborough's history and I am delighted that a film is to be made in celebration of it.'

Councillor Don Robinson was a member of the consortium which launched the radio ship in 1966.

Don Robinson said, 'This was a tremendous period. It was the 1960s - the peak of the rock era - and everyone was having a brilliant time. The pirate radio ship was an excellent experience.

At first we only thought listeners would be able to hear us in Yorkshire but in the end they could hear the station in Leicester, Nottingham and all over the Midlands.

I remember once the ship broke its mast and had to come to Scarborough for repairs - the response and interest it generated was unbelievable.'

Moves are now underway to find out whether the recreated ship which will be used to film the movie can be brought to Scarborough, as a tourist attraction, when shooting ends.

\*

In a separate report Paul Burnett, one time disc jockey on Radio 270 said: 'I finished working on Classic Gold last year to start work as a consultant on the film. Angus Deayton will play the part of a government guy trying to close down the station.

We have already done some pre-production work in Scarborough looking for suitable locations while the interiors for the film will be done in Belgium.

There will be a small cameo role for me. We are also thinking of having cameo roles for Tony Blackburn and Dave Lee Travis. The film will reflect a special time in people's lives when you suddenly had radio, but nothing to listen to.'

Mr Burnett said he would be looking forward to returning to Scarborough where he once had an apartment on South Cliff.

'I remember going for a drink in the old Pavilion Hotel and also meeting Don Robinson. He was a great guy,' said Mr Burnett.

Angus Deayton is well known as the former presenter of Have I Got News For You, Michael Gambon starred in the TV series Singing Detective and Richard E Grant starred in Withnail and I.

Hal Lindes, a former member of Dire Straits, is being recruited to organise the soundtrack to Making Waves featuring music from 1966-67 when Radio 270 was on the air.

The screenplay will be by Simon Nye who wrote the scripts for Men Behaving Badly. Ian Sharp, who directed episodes of Minder and The Professionals, is being lined up as the director.'

\*

NB: Unfortunately, we now understand that the production of the film has been held up indefinitely 'on financial grounds'.

# Little Richard – 14<sup>th</sup> May 1964

Whilst you or I might have been content to be involved with Flamingo Park, or with Radio 270, or be toying with wrestling, or rugby, Don Robinson was multi-tasking and as well as Flamingo Park and Radio 270 he was becoming a well- known and respected concert promoter.

On the 14th May 1964 he put on an 'all night dance' at Bridlington Spa. He tells me there were 10 bands and the dance ran from 8pm until 1am the following morning. The Spa was full, with Don says, a crowd of around 6,000.

The star who attracted that number was none other than Little Richard.

Whilst Don produced the following photo and confirmed he had booked the 10 bands and Little Richard, he could not remember the year or the date and had no press cuttings in confirmation. So we started investigating.

Bridlington Spa staff was very helpful but had no records going back that far. Neither are their past booking records digitalised. However, they confirmed from the photo that it had been taken at Bridlington Spa and they suggested I contact Sarah Hutchinson from Bridlington Library.

Only two days later Sarah replied to confirm that Little Richard had, in fact, played at Bridlington Spa on 14th May 1964 and that Don Robinson had promoted the "Mods' Ball' as the event had been advertised.

*Little Richard –Bridlington Spa, 14th May 1964*

She had contacted 'a few people' and also came up with the gems that 'Little Richard laid on the piano and played it backwards, possibly singing 'Hound Dog' at the same time,' and that, 'he wiped his face with small hand towels which he then threw down to the crowds'.

Not only that but one of her contacts had come back with, 'Little Richard did perform [at Bridlington Spa]. Gene Vincent also played there but I don't know if it was the same gig. Don Robinson Promotions from Scarborough brought the best artists to the Spa at that time.'

DON ROBINSON proudly presents

# BRIDLINGTON SPA ROYAL HALL
### THURSDAY 14th MAY
## ROCK, TWIST, AND STOMP
# MODS BALL
America's Top Recording and Television Star in person
"THE FABULOUS"
# LITTLE RICHARD
### with his backing group
# "THE FLINTSTONES"
plus the Mersey Sound of
## THE ESCORTS — THE FABULOUS McCOGS
## THE MOONSHOTS
LICENSED BARS —— REFRESHMENTS

# 8 p.m. to 1 a.m. Admission 10/-

Tickets now on sale at Bernard Deans, St. Thomas Street, Scarborough; Don Robinson's Managements Ltd., Westminster Bank Chambers. St. Nicholas Street, Scarborough, Tel. 6019 - 4059; Bridlington Spa Royal Hall.

## ALL TICKETS SOLD FOR THE ROLLING STONES
## REMEMBER TO BOOK EARLY FOR LITTLE RICHARD

Pip Waller from Scarborough remembers: 'I was there the night Little Richard played at Bridlington Spa. One of the supporting bands was The Moonshots and one of its members was called Robert Palmer. The Moonshots manager was Ron Gillette, maybe better known as a Cooperative Insurance agent in real life. Ron tended to use the Wimpy Bar on Northway as his office. Ron almost ran over Robert Palmer* in his car on Scarborough's sea front after Robert had dashed across the road. After the 'near-miss' they got talking, Ron recruited Robert into the Moonshots and, as they say, the rest is history.

*

*[Robert Allen Palmer (19 January 1949 – 26 September 2003) was an English singer-songwriter and musician. He first started with an amateur Scarborough based band called The Moonshots. He moved on and became known for his sharp dress sense and distinctive voice, and the eclectic mix of musical styles on his albums, combining soul, jazz, rock, pop, reggae and blues. He found success both in his solo career and with Power Station, and had Top 10 songs in both the UK and the US. His iconic music videos directed by British fashion photographer Terence Donovan for the hits 'Addicted to Love' and 'Simply Irresistible' featured identically dressed dancing women with pale faces, dark eye makeup and bright red lipstick, which resembled the women in the art of Patrick Nagel, an artist popular in the 1980s. Palmer's involvement in the music industry commenced in the 1960s, covered four decades and included a spell with Vinegar Joe.

Palmer received a number of awards throughout his career, including two Grammy Awards for Best Male Rock Vocal Performance, an MTV Video Music Award, and was twice nominated for the Brit Award for Best British Male.]

# CHAPTER 4

## 1965 - LAS VEGAS USA
## SCARBOROUGH ZOO AND MARINELAND
## MR MARVEL'S THEME PARK
## WATERSCENE, and
## IT'S A KNOCKOUT

So, after Don Robinson's excursion into offshore commercial radio and promoting Little Richard, what did he next get up to?

Whilst Ocean 7, alias Radio 270, was valiantly trying to cope with wild, windy and very wet weather in the North Sea, Don was looking for future ventures and turned his hand to organising the first direct air charter flight from England to Las Vegas, USA. He says this first flight, on a propeller driven plane, took 23 hours and had 4 refuelling stops in each direction, Iceland, Canada, East USA, mid USA then Las Vegas. Don says each return flight cost £94 guineas. Had he priced tickets in pounds the cost would have been over £100 – but that would have sounded more expensive! This flight was the first of 8 he ran over succeeding years although subsequent planes were early Boeing jets so the flight time was shorter and refuelling stops reduced.

These annual flights were arranged for members of the North Eastern Sporting Club (Newcastle) Limited, of which Don Robinson was chairman. The company had started life by running boxing shows at the Gosforth Park Hotel, Newcastle and its operations were later extended to promoting inclusive charter flights to the United States and the Far East.

BP

*'No - that's no snowman, that's Don!*

A Newcastle press report of November 1966 says,
'Mr William McKeag, Newcastle United Football director
and twice the city's Lord Mayor, together with Don
Robinson, Chairman of the North Eastern Sporting Club,
were both given a Key conveying the Freedom of the City
of Las Vegas during the club's week-long stay in the
gambling capital of the world.

The occasion had all the splendour you'd expect.

A brightly coloured police car screeched up to the
plush Thunderbird Hotel early one morning, and a
policeman jumped out to announce that he'd arrived for
the 'English party.'

Mr McKeag, and Don Robinson accompanied by
former Tyne and Wear soccer star, Len Shackleton and
John Gibson, were whisked away through the
jungle of casinos, sprawling hotels and wedding
chapels and into the presence of Mayor Grant Stewart
and City Manager Art. Trelease.

*Don Robinson is back right, behind William McKeag*

I should add that Sergeant Robert Behrman, our driver, is one of the most colourful characters I've ever met.

With a loaded pistol on his right hip, a cylinder of tear gas in his belt and a loaded shotgun strapped beside him in the car in case of riots, he looked like a one-man army.

Keys of Las Vegas were handed over to Mr McKeag and Don Robinson with typical American flourish - and then it was off on a whirlwind tour of the area with Sergeant Behrman.'

Don was only in his early 30s at the time of the presentation of the Las Vegas Key and he says, 'This was one of my proudest achievements although I am now also a Freeman of the City of London and also of my adopted home town Scarborough.

Recent recipients of the Las Vegas Key were film stars Michael Douglas and Robert de Niro for the film 'Last Vegas'.

# Scarborough Zoo and Marineland

A report in the Scarborough Evening News in 1969 announced the opening of Don Robinson's latest tourist attraction which he called Scarborough Zoo and Marineland.

'At the end of last year [1968] 7 acres of land overlooking the Open Air Theatre, in Northstead Manor Gardens, comprised about 40 tennis hard courts. Today the area has been transformed to the Zoo Park and Marineland, with an adjoining adventure playground for the children.

In 1968 Scarborough Zoo and Marineland Limited was incorporated and took a lease on a former tennis court site of 7 acres from Scarborough Corporation. The transformation was the idea of Scarborough entertainments promoter Mr Don Robinson, who a year or two ago saw the potential of the site. However, it was not until last year that he got permission to bring his plans to fruition and it was winter before work could start. The result is that the area is now gay with colour and can provide a full morning or afternoon's entertainment for the whole family.

The Zoo and Marineland boasts that once the customer has paid his or her entrance fee there are no hidden extras to pay. The fee covers everything, including seeing and feeding the animals and an almost non-stop series of small shows. Work started at Christmas, but because of the bad winter there were inevitable delays and towards the end it became a race against time to get the project open. It is to be formally opened tomorrow, but in fact it opened to the public last Sunday when 3,000 people went through the gates on that one day.

*Scarborough Zoo and Marineland*

A labour force of 35 worked to transform the area and made all the pools, pens, cages and buildings as well as the fibreglass Disneyland figures. During the operation 16,000 pieces of turf were lifted from an area behind Scarborough Hospital and taken to Northstead Manor Gardens to provide grassy areas.

Probably the most popular attraction will be two trick-performing dolphins flown to London from the US and then transported by road to Scarborough. They arrived this week but one of them has since died and Mr Robinson expects a replacement this weekend.

*[45 years ago there was demand from the public who wished to see live and performing animals 'in the flesh'. For most people that would be the only way to see them. Television was not as sophisticated as now, and scientific research was not available to give advice regarding the captivity of marine animals. Legislation was changed in the 1980's to increase pool sizes and it is now clear that dolphins can swim hundreds of miles a day so there no pool can possibly accommodate their needs. As knowledge increased and scientific research progressed this became realised in the UK in which there are now no Dolphinarium.]*

Sammy and Samantha are sea lions and Sammy achieved notoriety shortly after arriving in Scarborough from the US by escaping and swimming away in the North Sea. After three weeks at large he fell for the feminine charms of Samantha who was taken by road to Cleethorpes where Sammy was making occasional appearances.

No self-respecting zoo would be without a snake pit and Scarborough's new zoo is no exception. Sliding and slithering about in natural surroundings are 100 snakes and lizards. For those who find snakes unattractive, the chicken hatchery could make amends. In a six-sided building chickens can be seen hatching out each day and these always bring the 'oohs' and 'aahs' from the children

– and their parents! In another glass-windowed building rats and mice can be seen living above and below ground. Spectators can watch them as they go down and travel along tunnels to their dens. Add to this a baby elephant, wolves, bear cubs, llamas and a host of other animals and the whole is an interesting piece of entertainment. Flying squirrels, ground squirrels, chipmunks and other small animals are included. There is also a large aviary with varied birds – ranging from vultures and peacocks to Chinese oriental birds.

*Above and below: Picture postcards of the zoo.*

Marineland Amusement Park, Scarborough

In addition to all this there is a Fantasia Model Village where the visitor can wander through an acre of landscaped setting, in which there are different model houses. At a house the visitor presses a button and the figures start to move and a short story of about two minutes, with background music, is told. Another prominent feature of the zoo is the Noah's Ark, where multi-coloured lights illuminate various models and there is a story, with animated figures of an old toymaker whose toys come to life.

If one looks carefully, even the moustaches on the face of model soldiers can be seen to twitch.

Alongside the zoo is the Continental Adventure Playground, which in its first three or four weeks, attracted some 12,000 children. This boasts the longest slide – 145 feet – in Europe. It is 35 feet high and there are other attractions such as sputniks and other children's' amusements. The playground is another place where children could – and do – spend half a day, while their parents have a walk of just sit and watch.

The zoo was developed by business man Don Robinson who was also involved with Scotia Leisure, one time owners of Flamingo Park Zoo and its satellites. Scarborough later supplied dolphins for Don's Blair Drummond Safari Park in Scotland in which Jimmy Chipperfield of circus fame was also a director.

Don also had associations with the directors of Margate dolphinarium and other parks involved in dolphin displays at the time such as Gwrych Castle.

In 1970, Scotia Pleasure Parks Limited, the company which had taken over Flamingo Park Zoo, made a takeover bid for Scarborough Zoo and Marineland Limited. This bid was rejected but as a result of the negotiations Don Robinson was asked to run the Scotia Pleasure Parks Division covering Flamingo Park, Dudley, and various other zoos.

*Above: A 'Board meeting' with Don Robinson 2nd left.*

This, Don agreed, and the Scotia Pleasure Parks division, previously a loss making division, was converted to making a profit of £280,000 over a 3 year period.

In 1972 the company extended by opening a dolphinarium at Montreal Safari Park, Canada.'

Don Robinson commented recently:

'I do feel that it was important at that time for people to be able to see live animals. This was obviously decades before The Discovery Channel came into being and in those days television was much less sophisticated. Hopefully it was seeing marine animals in captivity which actually eventually stimulated interest and research into their welfare.

In hindsight it is easy to criticise but the reality was we were entering new territory and this was not even a topic of discussion at that time. Having seen the scientific research; having been involved in dolphinariums I am firmly of the belief that no marine animals should be allowed to perform and be kept in captivity and I think the UK has taken a strong lead on this issue globally.'

In 1973 Don Robinson Holdings Limited was formed to take over the various associated companies Don controlled. 65% of the share capital of Don Robinson Holdings Limited was then sold to Trident Television Limited – a company which controlled both Tyne Tees TV and Yorkshire TV – for cash and shares, valuing the company at £600,000.
Trident TV was majority shareholder but Don remained as Managing Director of Don Robinson Holdings Limited.

Again in 1973, with Don's fame spreading wider he was retained as a consultant to Great Adventure Amusement Park, New Jersey, United States, for staging of 'It's a Knockout'.

In 1977 Don sold his remaining 35% shareholding in Don Robinson Holdings Limited to Trident TV for £218,000. Windsor Safari Park Limited then came under the control of Trident Television Limited of which Don was appointed a director, but he resigned after 6 months because of disagreement over development policy. Subsequently Don and Sir Fred Pontin bought back Windsor Safari Park in 1983 when they bought the shell of Kunick. They closed Scarborough Zoo and Marineland in 1984 and the site was converted to Mr Marvel's Theme Park.

The tide was changing and animals in captivity were beginning to be frowned upon.'

*One of the chair lifts which took patrons to and from Zoo & Marineland, and, later Mr Marvel's*

## Mr Marvel's Theme Park

Situated at the top of the hill above Northstead Manor Gardens in Scarborough's North Bay - the same site previously occupied by the Zoo and Marineland - Marvels once boasted it had the largest roller coaster in Yorkshire. It was a Pinfari Zyklon coaster.

The park was served by two chair lifts and had dinosaurs, dodgems and entertainment of every description.

Whilst Don had converted Zoo and Marineland into Mr Marvels it had for a time been sold to Trident TV - with whom Don was director of the Leisure Division.

The Zoo and Marineland site which had developed into Mr Marvels Theme Park was then operated in 1987 until being sold in 1990. During this time Don's eldest son Nicky was manager.

Malcolm Stephenson was also involved in this period as managing director of Whitelands the controlling company.

In 1990 the Marvels site was sold into Edencorp Leisure PLC.

Then in 1992 the Marvels site was bought back and taken over by Malcolm Stephenson & Associates Ltd and run as Marvels Leisure until 2002 when the site was then released to enable the ensuing redevelopment, code named Zenith, to take over the whole area.

This had been planned by local businessman Malcolm Stephenson and was intended to completely renovate the North Bay and in particular provide an all-weather indoor attraction centred round a waterpark. Town houses, apartments and hotel, restoration of the existing chalets, new ones, and the full refurbishment of the Open Air Theatre and ancillary area was planned. Over the course of the next few years this development Zenith, had the name changed to North Bay Project to avoid confusion whenn the original chosen developer was replaced by Benchmark. Then Benchmark themselves, once established on site, wished to give their own name to the project which then became The Sands.

So far (2014) the two large apartment blocks have been built and the Open Air Theatre which provides concerts during the summer months, is up and running.

Unfortunately, as the country's financial difficulties have slowed down the development, Mr Marvels site has not yet been redeveloped.

Subsequently Scarborough Council bought back the lease prior to the expected redevelopment of the site as part of The Sands development. For various reasons the developers of the Sands were not able to proceed as quickly as planned and although all rides and most movable items were sold or removed by the previous leaseholder, the remaining parts were left and lack of development led to decay of the old Mr Marvel's site.

There has been online comment that Don Robinson should have ensured that Mr Marvel's site was completely cleared on closure. However, this comment is wide of the mark. Don had sold the site many years before it finally closed so then had no responsibility or control over it.

*

# The North Bay Bathing Pool, Waterscene, Water Splash World, Atlantis

Scarborough's South Bay bathing pool had opened just before World War I and its North Bay equivalent, although much smaller, opened in July 1938, just before the start of World War II. Both the North Bay and South Bay Pools were closed to the public during the war years when the town was largely occupied by troops - although they might have been used towards training the many members of the armed forces stationed in the town.

*Bathing Pool, North Bay c1950, Scarborough*

The Frith Collection photo above, shows the pool around 1950 and below is an LNER railway advertisement which shows the pool to good effect.

The pool measured 250ft long and 60ft wide. It was a heated seawater pool, which swimmers originally paid one shilling (5p) to use.

**The pool then had various guises until it closed in 2007.**

In the 1960s demand for an indoor facility remained high so the council looked into covering the pool to create an indoor facility but concerns were expressed over running costs and this idea wasn't taken forward. Instead, in December 1967 a new £165,000 indoor swimming pool project was planned. Following financial support from both the public sector and local residents, work began on this indoor pool on Ryndle Crescent in the early 1970s. Scarborough Indoor Pool finally opened on Saturday 8th

January 1973 and remains open to this day with very little change.

Back to the North Bay Outdoor Pool and by 1984, despite attracting as many as 100,000 paying visitors a year, the Council claimed it had become a financial liability.

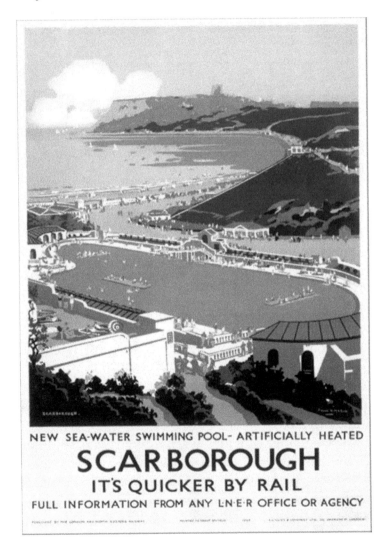

NEW SEA-WATER SWIMMING POOL- ARTIFICIALLY HEATED
# SCARBOROUGH
## IT'S QUICKER BY RAIL
### FULL INFORMATION FROM ANY L·N·E·R OFFICE OR AGENCY

Scarborough Council was forced to lease it out and it was taken over by Kunick Holdings, the entertainment company backed by local man Don Robinson and holiday king Sir Fred Pontin.

They updated the pool into a water theme park called Water Scene, and added two massive slides, said at one time to be the largest in Europe.

The Scarborough Evening News reported on 24th July 2009:

## Two Bathing Pools opened in Scarborough in 1984

*An aerial view of Water Scene after Don Robinson had installed the 'longest slides in Europe'.*

'One was a brand-new £200,000 pool in the Royal Hotel. The other was an upgraded North Bay pool, which had been renamed Water Scene by the Don Robinson company. Don Robinson was leasing the pool from the Borough council and had spent a reported £500,000 on upgrading it. The upgrading included two 165-metre-long water-chutes running down into the pool from the hillside behind. It was announced by Mr Robinson at this time that plans for the pool included a £300,000 River Run – with bathers able to shoot rapids on circular rubber rafts as they sped down a big chute to the pool.'

In 1987 the pool was sold on by Kunick to a company called Kirkpool and they renamed the attraction Watersplash World. Kirkpool Limited was incorporated on the 8th August 1986 but only two years later in 1989 they sold on the lease to London-based Edencorp. Edencorp went into administration in 1991.er rafts as they sped down a big chute to the pool.'

Scarborough Council bailiffs then took control of the site three months later, and the authority paid £202,000 in 1992 to get back the water park. It was re-launched as Atlantis in 1995 and remained popular with visitors and residents, and Council run until its closure in 2007.

The site has been earmarked for development as part of the North Bay Sands Development, and the council was in talks with developer Benchmark Leisure to establish a permanent use for it. Their proposal was a phased development which would replace the Corner Cafe site with two blocks of luxury apartments. The nearby derelict Open Air Theatre would be refurbished as phase two, and Atlantis would be demolished and an 'all season' water park constructed, as phase three.

Whilst Phases 1 and 2 have been undertaken, phase 3 has been agreed – but not on the old Atlantis site but in Burniston Road car park a few hundred yards away.

The old Atlantis site became untidy, unloved and derelict and the Council agreed a short term let to Crazy Combat Ltd - who already run similar attractions at Primrose Valley and Flamingoland. They provided a Military Adventure Park, featuring a miniature tank driving course, a laser tag shooting game, and inflatable challenges.'

## It's a Knockout

The Corporation ran events they called Aquatic Galas in the lake at the Open Air Theatre in Scarborough each Wednesday evening for many years. On Mondays and Thursdays the theatre had Light Opera performances with the principals being professionals but upwards of 200 amateur singers and ballet dancers filling the then vast stage which comprised the whole of the island frontage. The following evenings, Tuesdays and Fridays each week, were reserved in case the earlier performances were rained off before the interval in which case the audience got free tickets for the following night. If the show was rained off after the interval it was hard luck. There was no refund and no second performance.

The Council's Aquatic Galas were 'running out of steam,' Don says, so he offered to put on what he called 'It's a Knockout'. This was then a completely new concept and I feel it is fair to say that Don's idea of opposing teams who had to carry out all sorts of water and land based tasks to determine the winner, was the forerunner of a popular BBC TV show in the UK and throughout Europe of a similar name.

There were barrel races and pillow fights in the water, greasy poles to see how far along the pole contestants could crawl before falling into the lake and so on. These weekly events lasted 11 years until the original theatre closed in 1987.

Scarborough Amateur Swimming Club also assisted and one member recalls 'sacks full' of chemicals being heaped into the lake each Wednesday morning before the evening show to 'protect' the health of the swimmers.

Pip Waller recalls: 'I was based at RAF Fylingdales and I had returned from a posting to Cyprus and was on home leave before leaving for Ascension Island. We had two Australian members of the police staying with us in Scarborough and where better to take them for entertainment than Don's It's a Knockout at the Northstead Manor Gardens? When we arrived we saw that all ticket holders were being given a bingo ticket with a prize of a mini car for the winner. At the interval Don Robinson strolled out on to the grassed area at the right of the island stage and where the firework display would later be held.

He had a microphone and announced that he was going to call out the bingo numbers one by one and a single winner would win a prize of a mini car. He started to call out the numbers and as people ticked them off excitement started to build up. It got to the stage where very few numbers were left and people were thinking they were in with a chance of winning a car. He called out a few more numbers then all of a sudden 6000 members of the public simultaneously yelled "Bingo". The tickets were either all identical or were rigged so that the last number he called gave all 6,000 present, a full house.

To say the joke brought the house down would be an understatement!

Not only did Don Robinson put on these 'It's a Knockout' shows in Scarborough but when they took off he expanded them to Blackpool and Morecambe until 1979.

*

A Scarborough Open Air Theatre unofficial house record of 11,000 was claimed for a free entry recording of the BBC version of 'It's a Knockout' in the 1960s.

The BBC's televised shows were originally presented by McDonald Hobley, but he stayed for just one season before handing over to Katie Boyle, who in turn was replaced by David Vine and Eddie Waring. It was not until 1971 that the presenter most associated with the role, Stuart Hall, took over presenting the UK heats and also provided the British commentary for the international version along with Eddie Waring, who was better known as the BBC's Rugby League commentator.

On Sunday 14th August 1966 Scarborough was drawn against Bridlington at the Scarborough Open Air Theatre in the BBC version of It's a Knockout. Bridlington won by 13 points to 5.

# CHAPTER 5

## 1965 -THE WRESTLING YEARS

In the world of professional wrestling there were two ponds. Don Robinson was a big fish in the one of these two wrestling ponds. Naturally, being Don, he was a very large, colourful and energetic fish. There were no half measures wherever Don was concerned.

One pond was an organisation called Joint Promotions. Joint Promotions was a nationwide group of promoters who worked co-operatively by carving the towns and cities of Britain into distinct territories and employing wrestlers under exclusive contract. The group began working together shortly after the war, but it was 1952 before the Joint Promotion organisation officially came into existence. An exclusive contract to present televised wrestling gave Joint Promotions and their wrestlers an advantage over their rivals. Wrestlers who worked for Joint Promotions were forbidden from simultaneously working for other promoters, known as independents or opposition.

Don Robinson was not part of Joint Promotions; he was an independent and whilst there is no doubt that Don's entrepreneurial skills would have benefited Joint Promotions it is hard to envisage this colourful and creative talent sitting comfortably on the board of a rather conservative organisation.

For the most part the independent promoters were every bit as good, and often better, than their Joint Promotion colleagues. They needed to be, because they did not have the power of television to showcase their wrestlers and attract fans to their shows. A group of independents did form their own organisation, the Wrestling Federation of Great Britain, which was an effort to present a respectable and organised face of wrestling to the public. Don Robinson was the Chairman of the Federation consisting of ten independent promoters.

Without the famous names of wrestling such as Mick McManus, Jackie Pallo and Les Kellett at their disposal Don Robinson and his Federation colleagues had to discover new ways of enticing wrestling fans through the doors. They did it by creating larger than life characters unimaginable, and unpalatable, to the staid Joint Promotions. They took a young Sikh wrestler, told him to let his straggly hair cover his face, wear fur anklets and a leopard skin cape and re-named him The Wild Man of Borneo. A little known Scot was re-branded as The Mighty Chang; an old timer donned a bowler hat and umbrella, Paul Lincoln created the mysterious Doctor Death and so on. Add to these, overseas stars such as Crusher Verdu, Ski Hi Lee, Stamping Jack Lasar and Ricky Starr, and new home grown talent that included Klondyke Bill, Bob Kirkwood and Johnny Saint. With this colourful cast of characters Don advertised his wrestling shows on large colourful posters, often with photos of his odd collection of characters that were much more flamboyant than his Joint Promotions competitors.

In the 1960s Don was constantly challenging Joint Promotions by putting on exciting wrestling shows with wrestlers who were more colourful and larger than life than could ever be seen on television. He promoted his biggest shows at Scarborough (twice a week in summer), Bradford, Hull, Leeds, Middlesbrough, and Newcastle, and numerous other smaller halls around the country. He made use of the biggest names available; such as World champion Mike Marino and visiting American Ski Hi Lee, as well as his home grown talent, Klondyke Bill and Toma

Hansom (his friend Tommy Hanson), and appeared himself as masked man Dr Death. Don was not the original Dr Death, and remains modest about his role as this famous masked man, but those who saw him in action have told us he was a very good Dr Death.

Don stood out as a wrestling promoter because he was the master showman with an unequalled ability to generate publicity.

*The Wrestling match Don promoted at Queen's Hall Leeds on 7ᵗʰ March 1964*

Take for instance, the wrestling show Don promoted at the Queen's Hall Leeds on 7th March 1964. The Queen's Hall was a cavernous arena, built in the early years of the twentieth century, and had begun life as a tram depot. Following the scrapping of Leeds trams in 1959 the depot in Swinegate was converted to an entertainment venue two years later.

Few independent promoters would have had the audacity or courage to promote wrestling in this large arena. A huge banner above the doorway of the hall announced the spectacular wrestling show with the main event being a World heavyweight championship contest. On the day advanced tickets went on sale a queue of around two hundred fans waited for the opening of the box office at 11.00 am. Even Don was astounded when he travelled to Leeds on the night of the show to find a massive queue snaking its way around the hall.

Never on television would wrestling fans have witnessed the show presented by Don that Saturday evening. With the lights in the hall lowered, the bright light above the ring shone down on the white canvas and through the darkness fans strained to see the strange looking man entering at the back of the hall. Making his way through the jeering fans, with the brave ones reaching out to touch him, was Quasimodo, a hunchbacked Spaniard dressed in green boots and jester's jacket. As he made his journey to the ring he would occasionally stop to snarl at the jeering fans, ring the large hand bell he was carrying, and claw at the air. The hunched shoulders, missing teeth and scary features made Quasimodo an inevitable villain, and he was not one to disappoint fans at the Queen's Hall that night. In the unwritten rules of wrestling his opponent just had to be a good guy, and that role fell to a popular youngster named Dave Larsen. These were pre-politically correct days and 'Twist, twist,' shouted the fans as heroic Dave grabbed hold of the cyst on Quasimodo's shaven head and gave it a good twist. Inevitably good overcame evil and young Dave caught Quasimodo to put him on the canvas for the required count of ten.

The three thousand fans present had no time to gain their breath before the show continued in similar style. Good ousted evil once again when the popular experienced Londoner Judo Al Hayes (he was to become a Conservative councillor shortly afterwards) defeated a muscular twenty stone tyrant known as The Mighty Chang. Both may well have been familiar faces to fans; Hayes because he had previously worked for the television promoters, and Chang for his long running appearances as a bodyguard in a well-known TV tobacco advertisement, and role of a villain in the 1962 James Bond film, Dr No.

The tradition of good vanquishing evil was temporarily suspended when the masked Doctor Death defeated the fans favourite, El Blanco, in a loser to unmask contest. Fans waited with anticipation as the strings of the mask were loosened and the face of another novice Federation wrestler, Bob Kirkwood, was revealed.

In many ways the passing of a half century seems to have delivered us to another planet. Such an example was the wrestling midgets. These days it would be socially unacceptable to laugh at the antics of two midgets who had little interest in wrestling, but were very skilled in following their well-rehearsed routines to amuse an appreciative public. There was little wrestling but lots of laughs as Tiny Tim Gallagher defeated Hard Boiled Fuzzy Kaye.

The real wrestling of the evening came in the main event, when two seasoned professionals of considerable skill, Mike Marino and Dai Sullivan, wrestled for Marino's World mid heavyweight championship, with fans' favourite Marino being the winner as anticipated.

Following all that, the evening was brought to a close with a tag team match, a style of wrestling imported from America in which teams of two wrestlers faced each other.

On such occasions fans expected a good versus evil encounter in which all four participants ended up in the ring. They were not disappointed as the Australian heavyweights Dennis Dean and Rebel Ray Hunter overcame the unlikely pairing of Society Boy, complete with bowler hat and umbrella, and The Wild Man of Borneo, the barefoot behemoth.

THE PLAZA · TYNEMOUTH

# WRESTLING

DOORS OPEN 7 P.M. **FRIDAY 17 JULY** COMMENCE 8 P.M.

THEY MEET AT LAST BY PUBLIC DEMAND!!

# BILLY RED CLOUD

POPULAR RED INDIAN WARRIOR

v

# DOCTOR DEATH

AMERICA'S MOST HATED WRESTLER

RAY 'DROP KICK' CLARKE v DON NUGENT

DICKY SWALES v JIMMY DEVLIN

• THE RETURN CONTEST YOU HAVE SPECIALLY ASKED FOR •

BUTCHER GOODMAN v PEDRO ROMANY

Not all wrestling venues could afford such extravagant shows. The norm was four contests with a mixture of famous and lesser known names. Where small towns could not support shows with the biggest names the ever entrepreneurial Don came up with a novel solution. On 5th February, 1963, when the American Ski Hi Lee wrestled Mike Marino at the Olympia Ballroom in Scarborough, Don arranged  for coaches to transport fans from the market town of Malton for 2s/6d (12.5d return).

One of the Don's workers was a man called Gordon Lythe.  He was a big man and Don saw potential for him in wrestling. He called him Klondyke Bill and he became a big star around Europe. The BBC even featured him in the documentary series, 'The Philpott Files'. Gordon weighed about 30 stones. On his debut wrestling match the steps broke as Klondyke climbed into the ring; he fell and was unable to continue. Don has always claimed it was a genuine accident; others in the business have told us they suspect the accident was planned as Klondyke was not ready to wrestle

*Don Robinson, left, with Klondyke Bill in the fur hat.*

Despite being a hard-nosed and very successful businessman Don has always remained true to his roots and treated others fairly and with respect. Steve Walton, the dolphin trainer at Marineland (and part time wrestler) talked of working for Don Robinson in the 1960s in terms of being part of a family. It is a family that has survived to the present day with Don maintaining close connections with colleagues from years ago. Tommy Hanson was a big part of that family and Tommy's death in 2013 was a huge loss. Steve Walton read the eulogy at the funeral, following which Don along with Tommy's granddaughters, ex-wrestlers Steve Walton, Les Prest and boxing champion Richard Dunn, went to sea to scatter Tommy's ashes.

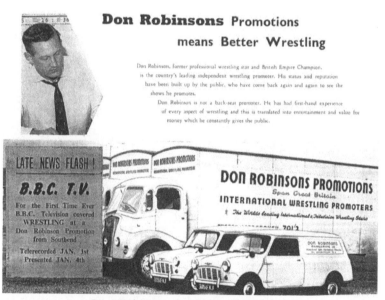

*Don Robinson Promotions advertisement*

Wrestlers are quick to complain about promoters, usually for a reluctance to pay travelling expenses or even the agreed fee due to an alleged poor attendance. Most wrestlers say Don was a fair man to work for who paid them reasonably. The one complaint they have about him is that he always paid them with a cheque - not good for them where the tax man was involved!

In 1957 the Chancellor of the Exchequer removed the entertainment tax. One year earlier Independent Television had begun broadcasting wrestling. By 1960 wrestling on television had become so popular that transmissions became weekly. Entrepreneurial Don Robinson was quick to recognise the financial opportunities of this growing sport.

Wrestling was certainly not Don Robinson's first love. Rugby was where his heart lay, and whilst playing for Hull Kingston Rovers he became friends with Sam Evans. Sam was nearing the end of his rugby playing career and already had his plans in place to turn to professional wrestling. No doubt Sam's friendship instilled an interest in wrestling, but his was not the only influence. Former wrestler Jimmy 'Boy' Devlin recalls leaving the ring following a match in Northallerton and being approached by two men. The two men were Don Robinson and Tommy Hanson, who told Jimmy they would like to speak to wrestler Jim Stockdale. Jim Stockdale was an experienced wrestler from Stockton who trained wrestlers at his gymnasium behind his father's public house, the Grey Horse. It was the start of a partnership with Jim Stockdale from which Don was to learn a great deal about wrestling and promoting. Jim Stockdale wasn't the only man from whom Don learned the business, and he attributes much of his knowledge to another Yorkshire man, veteran wrestler-promoter Cyril Knowles.

Don took wrestlers to Sweden, Finland and Bombay in India where they performed in the Sardar Patel Stadium which had a 50,000 audience capacity. The tour of Sweden, in 1967, was the first time professional wrestling had been held in Sweden for 25 years. Don wrestled on the shows, wearing a mask as Dr Death. One night a local wrestler jumped into the ring and challenged the hooded

Don to a fight. Not only were fans clamouring for the fight but the local media showed immense interest, even to the extent that their investigations traced Dr Death's origins back to Don's Scarborough home.

In April 1964 the BBC launched their second television channel, BBC2. For a brief moment the national broadcaster flirted with professional wrestling. On 4th January, 1965, wrestling was broadcast from Southend, and the man chosen to promote the tournament was Don Robinson. The programme had gone largely unnoticed as BBC2 was only available in London, the South East and Birmingham to those who had invested in a new aerial and a dual standard television set that could receive the new station broadcast on UHF 625 lines.

Broadcast at 7.00pm the BBC promised, 'An international competition of all-star wrestling from the Cliffs Pavilion, Southend, where some of Britain's leading wrestlers top the bill in a gala charity performance.'

Commentary was by Eddie Waring, at the request of Don himself, and Mike Marino faced 'Harlem' Jimmy Brown in the main event of the fund-raising show for the Variety Club of Great Britain. Also on the bill were Dai Sullivan, Gori Ed Mangotitch, Judo Al Hayes and Jimmy Devlin.

Devlin remembers the day well, 'We all thought this could be the start of something big, and that we would not look back. I was on with Milton Clarke, and I remember we got very good money for the match. Normally I would get £5 a match but for the BBC show I was paid 21 guineas (£22.05)'

Jimmy Devlin was right. This could have been the start of something big. Five months later BBC television embarked on a bolder experiment and for a fleeting moment on Monday 24th May 1965 it seemed possible that the world of professional wrestling may change forever.

As the time approached 10.15pm, just after Perry Mason had astonishingly won yet another apparently hopeless case, the BBC1 continuity announcer informed viewers that the following programme would be professional wrestling from the Sports Stadium, Brighton, an historic wrestling venue that had witnessed Lou Thesz defending his World Championship against Bill Verna a few years earlier.

Until that moment ITV and Joint Promotions had been the enclave of televised wrestling. With both Joint Promotions and independent television companies keen to protect the public image of wrestling as a competitive sport, viewers were familiar with highly regulated shows that were far less exciting and much more predictable than the wrestling that could be seen live in the halls of Britain.

The first national broadcast on the BBC offered the tantalising prospect of the beginning of a challenge to the dominance of ITV and Joint Promotions that would have changed professional wrestling for years to come. Within seconds of wrestling going over to 'the other side' it was clear that the BBC had fewer inhibitions about the reputation of professional wrestling than their commercial rivals. Unlike ITV the BBC show was produced by the light entertainment department and not BBC sports. Nevertheless, Eddie Waring was again enlisted to provide an irreverent commentary from the perspective of a respected sports commentator.

Those who saw the broadcast on their 19" black and white televisions remember that the more effective use of microphones around the hall improved the atmosphere in their living rooms and gave the programme more of a 'live' feeling than the ITV shows. Mind you, with more than 4,000 fans packed into the huge stadium there were enough present to make a lot of noise.

The wrestling itself was of a much rougher nature than that normally seen on television and viewers recall abuse of the referee, something that would never have been allowed on ITV.

Three bouts were broadcast over the following forty five minutes. The tempestuous Doncaster heavyweight Dai Sulivan faced the French wrestler Andre Drapp and in the main event Leeds heavyweight Jim Armstrong faced the former world heavyweight champion Eduard Carpentier. The third contest, the one which displayed the technical skills of the wrestlers, matched Sullivan's son Earl McCready with Londoner Tony Rocca. Two more matches, that were not broadcast, matched Peter Kelly with Tony Granzi and Chris Harris with Abe Goldstein.

The programme ended at 11.00pm, just in time for the news headlines. Suggestions made at the time - that the end of the contest had been conveniently arranged in time for the news - were nonsense as the matches had been recorded the previous Friday.

Unknown to viewers, and BBC executives, was that the Brighton show itself almost never took place. Behind the scenes was a tussle of two business giants greater than anything we might have seen in the ring.

Following the success of the earlier Southend show Don Robinson had high hopes that the BBC would award his company the rights to promote future shows for transmission. Headquartered in Westminster Bank Chambers, Scarborough, the company had recently expanded their promotional businesses into the south and shared the offices of Paul Lincoln Management in Old Compton Street, London.

It was a massive shock to Robinson when one of his wrestlers, Dai Sullivan, told him of a telegram he had received from Jarvis Astaire asking him to take part in a show he was promoting at Brighton for the BBC. Astaire was an entrepreneur with a vision of broadcasting closed circuit events around the world. He had already begun to develop a business portfolio that included wrestling promoting, as a vehicle for his broadcasting ambitions, and had many influential contacts in broadcasting and entertainment spheres.

Robinson advised Sullivan and the other wrestlers to telegram their agreement to appear for Astaire; knowing that a telegram would not be accepted as evidence in any legal proceedings that might follow.

On Friday 21st May, 1965, Robinson and the northern wrestlers billed to appear travelled to London and the offices of Jarvis Astaire. A blunt exchange of views took place in Astaire's office in which the Yorkshire man told Astaire the wrestlers would not be working for him that night and Astaire threatened legal action in return.

The discussions were at a stalemate until the moment Robinson told Astaire a group of wrestlers, including main eventer Jim Armstrong, were sitting in his car ready to return home and the telegrammed agreement to appear would hold no weight in court.

Astaire's response to the northern promoter's bravado was the moment that Robinson acquired a life-long admiration and respect for the more experienced business man he was facing.

Astaire, visibly shaken, remained completely in control of the situation and quietly suggested a break for coffee and sandwiches.

When the discussions resumed the atmosphere was completely different. Again Jarvis Astaire quietly assumed control and he calmly proposed that a positive solution be found to the impasse. An astute and experienced business man himself Don Robinson had already planned for this scenario; why else would he have brought the wrestlers with him had he not planned to strike a deal?

Robinson proposed that the Brighton bill went ahead as planned, with Astaire promoting, but that the two of them agreed to form a joint company to promote future BBC shows should the opportunity arise. Hands were shaken and a deal was done.

'Jarvis Astaire is one of the hardest, but one of the most honest and friendliest of men I have ever met,' said Don.

Following the deal between the two business men they travelled together from Astaire's office to Brighton for the evening's wrestling. Don continued, 'It was a life changing day. I considered myself a successful business man, but this was the first time I had been in a real executive board room. It was the first time I had travelled in a Rolls Royce. Later in life I would travel in lots of Rolls Royce's, helicopters, aeroplanes, and meet incredible people, but Jarvis Astaire changed my life. He's a fantastic man.'

Wrestling fans hoping that the BBC's interest in the sport would continue and provide an alternative source of wrestling entertainment were to be disappointed as the national broadcaster declared a lack of space in the schedules for further events.

The disappointment of the independent promoters, particularly those best placed to take advantage of the situation such as Paul Lincoln and Don Robinson, must have been even greater as they saw the opportunity of lucrative contracts fade away. For Lincoln, in particular, it was a severe blow as four years earlier discussions between the Lincoln organisation and independent television executives had reached their final stages before ITV made a last minute decision to award the evening mid-week session of televised wrestling to Joint Promotions who were the incumbents of the Saturday programme.

The disappointment was equally great for Don Robinson as his co-operation with Jarvis Astaire would have made them a formidable force in British wrestling that would undoubtedly have changed the wrestling landscape for years to come.

Despite quickly withdrawing from televised wrestling tournaments the BBC continued to show an interest in professional wrestling.

In 1972 the BBC documentary series, "The Philpott File," devoted an entire programme to the life and career of the Klondyke Brothers, one of them Don's former employee and wrestling discovery. It was remarkable that the BBC dedicated the best part of an hour's peak time viewing to a sport they did not televise, and two participants known only to fans of the independent promoters.

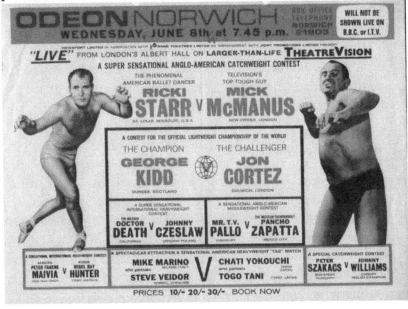

# 1976

Before Poland had left the Eastern block and joined Western Europe in 1986, promoter and manager Don Robinson took a team of wrestlers from the British Wrestling Federation to Poland.

*Greetings* from team manager Don Robinson and the British Wrestling Federation now touring Poland

Towards the end of the decade Don's wrestling interests in Britain began to dwindle until finally he concentrated his business activities elsewhere. Times were changing and the number of paying customers around the halls had begun to dwindle as fans became disenchanted with the tired routines they saw on television wrestling, still presented by Joint Promotions. Now if Don Robinson had been in charge ...

*[Hack and Anglo Italian of the Wrestling Heritage website kindly contributed to this chapter.]*

# CHAPTER 6

## 1970 - COLLEY'S CAMP

*Aerial photo of Colley's Cosy Camp at the end of Scholes Park Road, Scarborough, 1947. The seaward end of the camp is beyond the bottom of the photo.*

Colley's camp stretched back well before the start of World War 2 – certainly to the 1930's, and if the photo at the bottom of the next page does represent the camp, back to the 1920's.

Whilst Don Robinson was not directly involved in running this holiday camp he did buy it towards the end of its life as a camp and his present house is built on part of the camp site.

The camp provided budget accommodation for people wanting to get away for a holiday but not able to afford hotels or boarding houses.

COLLEY'S COSY CAMP • SCARBOROUGH

● 120,000 SATISFIED CUSTOMERS

Modern holiday camp set on gently sloping North Cliff overlooking sandy bay and Castle headland. Glorious sea views. Chalets with running h. and c., electric fires and cookers. Washing, ironing and drying rooms.

● FREE FIRST-CLASS ENTERTAINMENT PROGRAMME

Dancing to bands, cinema, giveaway with wonderful prizes and variety shows with top TV artistes. Children's shows and fancy dress. TV. Full Programme to suit all tastes. Licensed bar. Cafe. Snack Bar, Kiddies' Playground. Capacity 600 campers.

● SELF-CATERING

from 35/- per week according to season.

● FULL BOARD

from £6. 6s. per week. Reductions children. Special low pensioner terms.

OPEN MAY 15th TO SEPTEMBER 18th

3d. stamp for FREE Brochure and Tariff to
H. C. D. Colley's Cosy Camp, North Bay, Scarborough

The advert above – believed to be from the 1950s – says, the camp has had '120,000 satisfied customers, and a capacity of 600', that chalets have 'running h. and c. water, electric fires and cookers,' and that there was 'washing, ironing and drying rooms.' Self-catering terms were from 35/- (£1.75) per week, full board from £6/6s/0d (£6.30) per week and both included a 'Free First-Class Entertainment Programme.'

SCARBORO' HOLIDAY CAMP.

The photo on the previous page captioned 'Scarborough Holiday Camp' was taken in 1920 and could well have been Colley's Camp, as Scarborough Holiday Camp was an alternative name the camp used for advertising.

The two photos above were both taken in the mid-1950s, the top one showing what appears to be a sports day in progress.

John Forster recalls, 'Sometime in the late 1950s the camp caught fire spectacularly overnight, an event I watched from my bedroom window at 122 Scholes Park Road. The camp was rebuilt but many years later (c. early 1970s) was demolished and housing took its place.'

When Don Robinson bought the camp from the Colley family well over 40 years ago he demolished the old Colley family home then built his own present house on part of the camp site. He then did a deal with builder Peter Marshall whereby Marshall extended Don's drive and built a helipad adjoining the new house, then built flats on adjoining land. In part return Robinson conveyed part of what had been the Colley's large garden to Marshall.

James (later Lord) Hanson was a director of Trident TV and chairman of the Hanson Trust. Hanson had the use of a helicopter and had headhunted Don to run the Trident TV Leisure Division. Don had accepted and when he had to attend board meetings the helicopter used Don's helipad to land and collect him and this is depicted in the cartoon on the next page and on the cover.

Don says he was 'overawed when I first met Mr Hanson. This was someone whose fame and importance increased by leaps and bounds; someone who was knighted in 1976 and who was ennobled only 7 years later in 1983 and someone whose business in its heyday was worth more than £11bn. I was very proud to be associated with him.'

Trident was set up in August 1970 to deal with the problem of fairly allocating commercial airtime from a television transmitter at Bilsdale in North Yorkshire which straddled the catchment areas of two Independent Television companies. The transmitter itself was owned by the Independent Television Authority, the governing body of ITV. Due to the geographical nature of the area it served, allocating the transmitter to either of the two closest broadcasting companies, Yorkshire Television and Tyne Tees Television, would have given one an advantage over the other in terms of selling commercial airtime.

By October, the name 'Trident' was agreed, while shareholders in Yorkshire had agreed to the merger, with Yorkshire Chairman Sir Richard Graham becoming

Trident chairman and Yorkshire Managing Director Ward Thomas becoming MD at Trident. Mr Wilkinson and Mr James Hanson also joined the Trident board and Don Robinson later became a director of the Trident Leisure division.

In 1969, when Colley's camp was deserted during the winter months, the Sun newspaper, in its first ever edition had reported the following events, later featured in the Scarborough Evening News 40 years later:

# The day a wolf prowled loose in the North Bay...

Two wolves escaping from Scarborough's Zoo and Marineland made headline news in the first ever edition of The Sun newspaper in 1969.

To celebrate the paper's 40th anniversary this week, a copy of the first edition was reproduced in Monday's Sun.

Following on from a front page about racehorse doping, and speculation about the relationship between the then 21-year-old Prince Charles and Lady Leonora Grosvenor, was a page three story about a wolf hunt in Scarborough.

Under the headline 'Shots End Nightmare Wolf Hunt' was the tale of how two North American timber wolves escaped from their Zoo and Marineland pen on the morning of Sunday November 16th 1969:

The Zoo and Marineland, owned by Don Robinson, was a hugely popular attraction in Northstead Manor Gardens, on a site which would later become Mr Marvels' fun park. It included animals such as bears and dolphins, and funfair rides. Although one of the wolves was shot on site by the zoo's curator Keith Reaney, the other escaped, fleeing towards Scalby Mills.

Mr Reaney told the Evening News at the time that he thought someone had broken into the zoo the previous night because the lock on the wolf cage was missing. He had seen the escaped wolves roaming the grounds and unsuccessfully tried to shepherd them into the zoo workshop. When that failed he shot one but the other escaped over the perimeter fence.

Around 20 policemen, some of them armed, then took part in a three-hour hunt for the missing wolf, warning golfers at North Cliff and alerting anglers fishing off the North Bay promenade.

Sgt Kenneth Watson, then 42, was the officer to come across what was described in The Sun as 'the snarling wolf', as he searched the empty Colley's Holiday Camp, in Scalby Mills Road. In an interview with the Evening News, Sgt Watson said: 'I had come all the way from Scalby along the river bank, through the woods, and all the rest was open country. I came round the corner of a caravan in the camp and there was the wolf, heading my way. It was a case of shooting it or losing it.'

Sgt Watson used six shots from his 0.22 rifle before the wolf died.'

# CHAPTER 7

# 1973-2012 - THE COUNCIL YEARS

Whilst this chapter includes events in which Don Robinson was involved when a Scarborough Councillor, (1973 – 1983; 1999-2003) it also includes local matters on which he commented or was involved, from both before and after the time he was a Councillor.

Don first stood for Scarborough Borough Council and was elected as Conservative Councillor for Scarborough's Castle Ward on 7th June 1973. He remained a councillor until the 5th May 1983 election when he did not stand. 16 years later he again stood and was elected in 1999 remaining until 2003.

Between1979-1982 he was a member of the Hull University Court as the council representative.

Between 1980 and 1981 he was on the Scarborough Harbour committee, and between 1981 and 1982 the Finance sub-committee, Scarborough Harbour committee, and the Development Control committee (Central Urban).

Between 1999 and 2000 he was on the Personnel and Resources committee, Chairman of Scarborough Harbour committee, was a member of the Appeals committee, the Audit committee, and the Tourism committee. He did not stand for re-election in 2003.

Whilst on the Harbour committee he was responsible for ensuring that the harbour was dredged to allow more berths for leisure purposes. As a result Scarborough harbour and marina underwent a major regeneration including the new Albert Strange Pontoons, a more pedestrian-friendly promenade, street lighting and seating.

The more recent improvements to the inner harbour with the installation of pontoons to accommodate 60 permanent berths transformed the Sandside area. Along with complimentary land-based improvements such as the resurfacing of footpaths and implementing contemporary seating and lighting, the marina area is now a stunning asset of the town.

One wonders how a man, so intensely involved with a large portfolio of business affairs, companies and plc's, not only in Scarborough but by then throughout the country, could have made time to be part of the Borough Council. I think the answer was that he loved Scarborough his adopted town and at all times he wanted the very best for it.

However Don doesn't suffer fools gladly and he did get frustrated at what appeared to him to be lack of positive action by many councillors. He also felt strongly, and voiced his views strongly, that 47 Councillors for 25 Wards – some wards with 2 or even three councillors, was grossly excessive and that ratepayers' money could be saved by cutting down on numbers so each Ward had only one councillor.

Councillors' pay and pensions was another bone of contention.

He does feel now however, that Scarborough Council Leader Tom Fox is 'doing an excellent job in difficult circumstances and officers are some of the best the Council has had for a long time.'

# 1971

'An organisation dedicated to extending Scarborough's season was reactivated 35 years ago after being dormant for many years.

The Scarborough Townsmen's Association had done much in the way of promoting events to attract visitors outside the high season.

One of the prime movers was businessman Don Robinson. The new chairman was Rowland Curtis, the managing director of Futurist Enterprises.

One of its first moves was to take over the running of a Scarborough publicity coach which visited inland towns and cities in the off-season to promote tourism.'

## 1981 - Carnival

'Scarborough's first September Carnival in 1981 went with a bang, with four impressive firework displays.

Planning had gone on for most of the year, the aim being to boost the late season in the same way that the Dutch Festivals and their successors in June helped the early season.

But whereas the June festivals have been mounted each year since 1958 by the borough council, the September Carnival was the work largely of business people and others.

The first weekend included two firework displays from the castle headland, camel racing on the south sands, then a carnival parade plus a torchlight procession by children to a bonfire at Scalby Mills. The second saw jazz bands and drum majorettes at the North Marine Road cricket ground, The Great Yorkshire Fun Marathon and more fireworks from the castle.

Don Robinson, the Carnival instigator, said that Scarborough's September fireworks would soon be as famous as Blackpool's illuminations. The event was opened by Richard Whiteley of Yorkshire TV's Calendar programme.'

# 1984 – International Tennis

'International tennis could again have been on Scarborough's sporting calendar.

Plans by businessman Don Robinson to revive Scarborough as a top-class tennis venue will be discussed by Scarborough councillors at the Leisure and Amenities Committee meeting in nine days' time.

Robinson wants the dilapidated centre courts in Filey Road to be spruced up to host major tennis tournaments involving the current stars of the game.

He said that ideally he envisaged a competition being staged at Scarborough in the week after the world's top event - Wimbledon - when the sport's leading players are in Britain and interest in tennis is at its peak.

Robinson said that he saw little problem in attracting both sponsorship and television coverage of a Scarborough tournament.

He said: 'National sponsorship is available for such a competition. Tennis is big business these days. Wimbledon made more than £4m this year."

Robinson maintained that Scarborough could once again be a major base for tennis in Britain.

'The North of England is ready for a major tennis tournament, whether it's in Scarborough or elsewhere. Scarborough has got that chance," he said. He will be a guest at the Lawn Tennis Association's awards night at Harrogate — held in the North for the first time — on Saturday.

Robinson is determined to relaunch the courts in Filey Road to top level after their fall from grace in the late 1960s.

Until then Scarborough had enjoyed an envied reputation as Yorkshire's premier tennis venue, attracting such legends as Rod Laver, Ken Rosewall,

Pancho Gonzales, and Fred Perry.

But service at the courts was halted, ironically as sponsorship began to creep into the game. The North of England Championships were held for the last time in 1967, and it is 13 years since the Yorkshire championships were staged at the Filey Road courts.

Scarborough Council's Director of Tourism and Amenities David Elliott confirmed that the 'anyone for tennis' plan had been put on the committee agenda after he had had preliminary talks with Robinson.

Elliott said the courts were owned by Scarborough Council and leased to the Scarborough Lawn Tennis Club.

If the plans got the backing of Councillors he believed that the Scarborough LTC would continue to use the courts when tournaments were not being staged.'

## 1993 - Russian Warship Coming?
## 1993 - Floating Museums Proposal

'Not just one, but two floating museums for Scarborough Harbour were proposed in March 1993. One suggested venture was to moor an ex-Russian Navy frigate in the inner harbour and turn it into a World War II museum. It was proposed by Scarborough businessmen John Barman, and Don Robinson. The latter already had a wartime museum – the Winston Churchill Britain at War attraction in London. They were proposing to invest £750,000 in the venture and ideally wanted to berth the 1980 vessel alongside the North Wharf.

The other venture was proposed by the Pindar printing firm. The vessel it had in mind was a former trawler called the Hatherleigh which had become an oil-rig stand-by vessel and was then based at Lowestoft.

Pindar's said they would turn the ship into a museum of the maritime history of Scarborough, particularly the history of its fishing industry, and that they would like to have the vessel moored in the inner harbour alongside the middle pier.

# THE RUSSIAN IS COMING!

*13 MAR 1993*

## Second plan for Scarboro' floating ship museum

EXCITING new plans have been unveiled to bring a Russian warship to Scarborough harbour to convert into a second floating museum.

The move comes only days after the Evening News revealed that a scheme has been launched to create a museum at the harbour based on the maritime history of Scarborough.

### Educational

Now two local businessmen, Don Robinson and John Barman, have stepped in with their own project to bring thousands of holidaymakers into the town.

They aim to invest around £750,000 in

**EXCLUSIVE**
by CHRIS NIXON

the museum which would be themed on the Second World War.

Mr Barman said: "We are looking at bringing a Russian frigate to Scarborough.

"It was only built in the early 1980s, but the Russians are looking at selling some of their vessels.

"The ship would also have an educational value, particularly as the war is now part of the national curriculum. .

"The warship would be an incredible attraction."

Mr Robinson said there was no reason

why his warship museum could not operate in the harbour as well as the maritime museum.

It was hoped that the warship could be tied up at the North Wharf, he said. There would be various attractions on the warship.

### War museum

The maritime museum would be developed on a former trawler, the Hatherleigh, presently based at Lowestoft. It would be moored at Vincent Pier.

The idea was put forward by Scarborough print firm GA Pindar and Son. Mr Robinson owns the Winston Churchill Britain At War Museum in London.

He welcomed the move by Henry Marshall to open the Scarborough Millennium in Sandside, which would display 1,000 years of the town's history.

DON ROBINSON: Hoping to bring a Russian warship to Scarborough harbour as a museum.

They added that the ship would also be used at times for Pindar corporate events,
and that on occasion it would sail to other ports to host gatherings for the company.

The Town Hall was cool about the Soviet warship idea. A report to councillors by a senior officer doubted if there was the enough custom at the harbour for two floating museums.'

## 1998 – Duelling A64 Road

'In 1998 Don Robinson strongly supported the Scarborough Evening News' Appeal to duel the rest of the A64 from York to Scarborough. Don had been chairman of the successful Malton bypass committee built in the 1970s and he felt that without the dual carriage way being extended all the way to Scarborough, the town could die.'

## 2000 - Zenith Fears

'Council chiefs fear the Zenith project [the initial project to redevelop and revitalise the north side of the town proposed and planned by businessman Malcolm Stephenson] could become caught in a Catch 22 situation.

The Evening News last week revealed a timetable has been set to try and force progress on the £250m scheme with the aim being to try and get financial backing and planning consent in place by the end of the summer at the latest.

But at a meeting of the policy and resources committee concerns were raised about just what could be achieved by then.

And it was hoped Zenith would not be trapped between the need to get permissions in place and attracting potential operators.

Coun Don Robinson said: 'Without operators interested this simply can't work, and after five years there doesn't appear to be any big names.

But we do realise that it can be difficult to attract this interest until planning permission and development costs have first been secured.'

Chairman Councillor Eileen Bosomworth urged time and space for officers to work alongside developer Grayling Sports and Leisure Ltd.

She added: 'It is a crucial time for Zenith and we are trying to forge ahead, but it isn't something which can just happen overnight.'

It was again stated that a major property company was very involved in negotiations to get the project back on track.

Chief executive John Trebble confirmed discussions were taking place, but said it was too commercially sensitive to reveal a name.

If we come to the point where we are able to sign a deal, then that is the time to make it public, he said. We have come a long way and achieved a great deal, but much more needs to be done, and that is what we are making sure happens.

Councillors agreed to the basic timetable laid out for Grayling, which means a planning application is wanted by August.

Shopping and transport reports, land deals and guarantees of financial backing must also be ready, or Zenith could face a grim future.

Speaking today, Scarborough businessman Malcolm Stephenson, the man who dreamt up the Zenith project, agreed it was in a Catch 22 position.

He added: 'There are plenty of people who are interested but no-one will commit themselves until outline planning permission is granted.

But I'm confident Grayling will meet the deadlines set by the council."

## 2000 - Pledge over plan to close Museum

'The leader of Scarborough Council has stepped in to protect the future of Scarborough's Wood End Museum and Filey Sun Lounge.

Cllr Eileen Bosomworth, who says she was not told about the planned closures, said they would not close in the foreseeable future and the proposals would be among the first things discussed by the council's new 10-strong cabinet in January.

The pledge came during a meeting of the council's policy and resources committee when members agreed to look again at proposed cuts to tourism and leisure services.

Plans to cut the opening hours at Atlantis Water Park could also be reversed.

The initial suggested cuts were approved in principle at last month's meeting of the council's tourism and leisure services committee, subject to a further report on their implications.

Mrs Bosomworth said the report did not have her support, adding that some of the savings would cause great problems for locals and holidaymakers.

Cllr Don Robinson said: 'I am very, very surprised you didn't know about this as leader of the council.'

Referring to Peter Dahl, the council's director of tourism, Mrs Bosomworth replied: 'The director let me down in not keeping me informed about this report. Some of the proposals have caused a tremendous amount of consternation. To the people who treasure Wood End I say there will not be closure in the foreseeable future.'

Members agreed several of the proposed cuts, including those affecting Wood End, Atlantis and Filey Sun Lounge, should be discussed by the council's cabinet in the New Year.

Councillors have already been told Atlantis lost £200,000 this year and some members thought the local authority should look at leasing it to private enterprise in the short-term pending a decision on the future of the Zenith project.

Cllr Michael Pitts said it would not be easy to find someone to take over Atlantis temporarily. The only people who had been interested had wanted a council subsidy.

He found support from Cllr Jane Kenyon who pointed out the difficulties the council had faced when it had previously had to take back control of Atlantis from a private operator.

We had to spend a lot of money to reopen it and bring it up to scratch, she said. The council took the view it was a prime site for tourism. If we had left it empty and derelict it would have sent out an appalling message.'

## 2000 - Call for action over rubbish filled pond

A leading councillor has called for the clean-up of a Scarborough pond which is filled with rubbish, including four dumped supermarket trolleys.

One resident said she complained about the state of the larger pond underneath Valley Bridge more than a year ago, but it is still in a state.

Today a senior Scarborough council officer promised an immediate clean-up when he was contacted by the Evening News.

Cllr Don Robinson, who has become a champion of the untidy public gardens campaign, said it was appalling that residents and visitors alike should be confronted by such a sight.

'This is the height of the season and this should be checked regularly', he said.

'We need at least 30 extra gardeners to sort out the open areas in the borough and the only way to put this in place is with good management and financial controls'.

Pensioner Elfreda Jones, of Grosvenor Road, said: 'I originally brought it to light in Easter 1999, and again this year, and the council officers said it was regularly cleaned out but I have never seen it happening and I live very nearby.

It is awful for holidaymakers to see it in such a mess and sometimes it smells atrocious. I know people should not throw things in it but this is on a tourist route and the council should keep it clean.'

Council spokesman Kevin Allen promised: 'All the trolleys and obvious rubbish will be removed today. We would like to clean it out completely but we do not have the money to spend at the moment. I estimate it would cost about £40,000 to do it properly, which would mean removing all the silt and re-sealing the pond.

It was last cleaned out properly four or five years ago and we put in a bid for cash for a major restoration project, in the Valley Road area, but we did not get it.'

## 2002 - You're killing Scarborough

'Dual the A64 or you will kill Scarborough. That was the message to the Highways Agency from Scarborough councillors.

They told the agency the lack of a dual carriageway linking the town with the rest of the country is strangling industry and destroying tourism.

Highways Agency officials said the forthcoming 10-year strategy for the A64 cannot include plans for an upgrade.

Councillors said public consultation to draw up the strategy was a waste of time and money.

At a meeting between councillors and agency officials yesterday Cllr Don Robinson said: 'This town is dying. It is being killed by the roads. If you don't upgrade the road you will kill Scarborough, you will kill the boarding houses, the factories and hotels.'

Leader of the council Cllr Eileen Bosomworth said: 'We have been let down for so many years with so many promises that have not been fulfilled.'

The cost of dualling the A64 between York and Scarborough has been estimated at more than £100 million.

Councillors believe it would be a small price to pay for the benefits it would bring.

'You are talking about a cost in the region of two or three decent premier league football players against this area becoming a blackspot for employment,' said Cllr Tony Randerson.

Highways Agency project manager for the strategy, David Phillips, said: 'It is not within the Highways Agency's power to say whether we will or will not dual the A64.'

The A64 route management strategy will not be completed for a number of months but it is likely to include a number of small scale improvements costing between £10 million and £12 million.'

## 2005 - Ideas to cut costs

'Further to our local council requesting ideas for reducing expenses to make up a £1.9 million shortfall, to start with how about taking up Cllr Don Robinson's recent suggestion to reduce the number of councillors, or would this ruffle too many feathers?

I have lived at the address below for 18 months, and I understand that the ward has three councillors.

I only found this information by going to the local library, otherwise I would not have seen or heard from them, presumably until just prior to election time.

I am sure other wards are simultaneously staffed, if the constituents made inquiries.

R B
Scarborough

## 2005 – Councillor Restrictions

Don Robinson's strong views about the number of councillors (he has support for his view that 1 councillor is adequate for each of the 25 Wards in Scarborough District rather than the present 47 councillors) and the fact that they receive generous allowances and pensions when council work was always before, a voluntary unpaid role, cannot have endeared him to some members of the Council. However it seems (March 2014) that his views have been listened to nationally and councillor pensions are to cease at the end of each current councillor's 4 year term. Newly elected councillors will not receive pensions.

The following correspondence in the Scarborough Evening News reflected Don's earlier views:

'I couldn't agree more with Don Robinson's comments as far as they go.

But I would suggest even more stringent reforms to the present set-up.

I think it would also be a good idea to limit a person to no more than two consecutive terms as an elected member and subject them to mandatory retirement at normal retirement age. After all it's a paid job with a pension. This would automatically make way for new blood and maybe a more dynamic approach to local problems and policies.

There should also be some form of qualification available to prove their fitness to run a multi-million pound business efficiently and effectively.

This is a must before you start paying them any more money. At the moment it appears to be an exclusive club of very limited membership with no membership fees where members can indulge themselves without any accountability.

They get attendance, subsistence and travelling allowances. If money runs short then they simply increase the council tax.

What about a referendum on above inflation council tax increases?'

(Name and address supplied)

'Even though it has involved greater expenditure, the extra improvements below the Town Hall and to the seafront are very worthwhile.

This is a well-used route, drawing people who stop to admire the view from the Queen Victoria statue, or who want a quicker route from the seafront to the town centre.

There are a lot of steps, and mums with pushchairs will still have to negotiate le Mans type bends, but the new scheme looks excellent.

The work was made inevitable because people had, understandably, created their own short-cut. It was proof that designers and landscapers cannot beat human nature.

But the problem was the muddy path that developed precisely because of the popularity of the shortcut.

Scarborough legend Don Robinson has been proved right. He said the original scheme was very good but flawed and he spotted the mess.

It's good news for everyone that action has been taken.'

(Name and address supplied)

## 2008 – Biggest Earthquake

'Terrified residents say they thought Scarborough had been struck by a hurricane after the town felt shockwaves from the most powerful earthquake to hit the UK in 25 years.

The tremor, measuring 5.3 on the Richter Scale, was felt just before 1am yesterday. It rattled windows and furniture and woke many people from their sleep.

A spokesman for North Yorkshire Police said: "We received a large number of calls about the earthquake but none relating to significant damage."

North Yorkshire Fire and Rescue says it was not called out to any emergencies in Scarborough but the

Humberside emergency services said it received 200 calls from people wanting to know what was happening.

The Scarborough Evening News was also inundated with phone calls and emails.

Scarborough businessman Don Robinson, of Scalby Mills Road, felt the tremor, but did not realise what it was until he received a phone call from friends in Spain. He said: 'It was very surprising – our friends said they had been watching the news and seen that there had been an earthquake in the UK. It did wake us at the time and we thought a hurricane had hit the coast. It shook the house and then it just went quiet.'

Teacher Pat Argent, 48, of Fulford Road, said: 'You couldn't quite believe what was happening. I have a pet budgie and two cockatiels and they went frantic. This is something that doesn't often happen in Scarborough!"

## 2008 - Festival would be a crowd-puller

'Entrepreneur Don Robinson – who has suggested an annual Scarborough Firework Festival – is someone well worth listening to on the subject of pyrotechnic displays and their crowd-pulling power.

His suggestion – made in our readers' letters columns – is that a big firework festival should be held on the Friday, Saturday and Sunday evenings of the Late Summer Bank Holiday Cricket Festival weekend.

In his earlier days, Mr Robinson was involved with some very spectacular firework displays in Scarborough. Early on, as a competitive swimmer, he got close-up views of the displays which closed Scarborough Amateur Swimming Club's weekly aquatic galas during the summer at the Open Air Theatre.

Years later, when he was presenting his popular weekly It's A Knockout shows at the Open Air Theatre during the summer, spectacular firework displays similarly closed the events.

And when he was prominent in helping to organise Late Summer Carnivals in Scarborough in the 1980s, big firework displays were again a feature.

These latter displays were all the more spectacular for being given from the top of the Castle Hill, with crowds lining the clifftops in both bays to see the colourful pyrotechnics over the sea.

Mr Robinson believes that, with the right promotion, a really ambitious Scarborough Firework Festival could soon outstrip the Blackpool illuminations as a crowd-puller. And it would be a brave person who would argue about crowd-pulling power with a man with his track record in that department.'

## 2010 - Fresh calls for upgrade of A64

'A Scarborough businessman has backed calls for a multi-million pound development of the A64 which he believes would return the town to its former status as the country's number one seaside resort.

Don Robinson, who owned The Zoo and Marineland attraction, said the whole route needed updating with the introduction of a dual carriageway into Scarborough and a new bypass around Rillington, which could potentially cost around £400 million.

Mr Robinson told the Evening News: 'Scarborough is being left behind and is in the wilderness in terms of the road structure. When visitors come to the town in the summer the road from when you get just past Malton is atrocious.

Scarborough was the number one resort in years gone by, but it seems we are being left behind, which is a shame because to my mind the town is still one of the best places around.

When the Scarborough cricket festival is on the road is just blocked with people and there needs to be something put in place to help traffic get to the town and support one of the town's potential gold mines too."

Mr Robinson, who is the founder of the Winston Churchill's Britain at War Experience in London, has received support from the town's MP Robert Goodwill, and said the introduction of the Malton bypass had set a precedent.

Mr Goodwill said he was looking into the situation and supported the call for potential work to take place.

He said: "A scheme to upgrade the whole road in one go, costing in excess of £400 million, may be difficult to achieve, but the approach of trying to do a bit at a time, as has already happened to some extent, could be the best way forward.

I have had conversations with Theresa Villiers, the Shadow Secretary of State for Transport, and she is never in any doubt of the importance I attach to the A64. It is very important as a means of securing the economic regeneration.'

## 2010 Theatre renovation worth singing about

'People in Scarborough have fond memories of the original Open Air Theatre – and its restoration was welcomed at yesterday's press conference to announce the opening acts.

It was confirmed that opera superstars Dame Kiri Te Kanawa and Jose Carreras would be performing together for the first time on a UK stage in Scarborough on Friday July 23.

Businessman Don Robinson, who used to run the popular It's a Knockout shows at the original venue during the 1970s and 1980s, said that Scarborough was currently undergoing a renaissance and the restoration of the Open Air Theatre was an important part of it.

He said: 'This is the best thing that's happened to Scarborough in the last 50 years. A lot of money has been spent on it but it'll bring a lot of people to Scarborough and it's going to get a lot of national and international publicity.'

Mr Robinson said individual developments – such as the renovation work at the Spa Complex, the Sands and the new eye-catching North Bay chalets – would all combine to make Scarborough the top tourist destination ahead of resorts such as Blackpool.

Cllr Bill Chatt, the Mayor of Scarborough, said it was an important part of the town's regeneration. He added: 'People will come to this town and spend their money.'

He added that he remembered the uncomfortable concrete surfaces of the original Open Air Theatre. He said: 'We used to rent cushions to try and make it more bearable. If it rained you got wet – but people didn't care because the most important thing was we got entertained.'

Scarborough comedian and impresario Tony Peers said the venue was a fantastic asset for Scarborough.

He added: 'I think the opening night will be a night to remember. Two of probably the biggest stars in the world here in this resort – how much better can it be? As someone who was part of the last show here, to see it come back to life again is simply wonderful.'

Cllr Janet Jefferson, Scarborough Council's portfolio holder for tourism and culture, said she remembered the original Open Air Theatre and yesterday's announcement was good news for Scarborough. She said: 'To have some international acts is a dream come true and it will boost our economy tremendously.'

Council leader, Cllr Tom Fox, added: 'I think it's absolutely fantastic and a reflection on what's to come, not only for the rest of the season but for years to come.'

He added that the restored Open Air Theatre would make Scarborough a destination in its own right for iconic shows and also boost the tourist trade.

John Senior, the chairman of the Scarborough South Bay Traders Association, added: 'This will be an amazing venue. It's been a long time in coming and we are delighted that this has been brought back to life."

## 2011- Television star David Jason says Scarborough is the best in Britain for seafood

The star of 'A Touch of Frost' and 'Only Fools and Horses', popped into Ocean's Pantry on West Pier with a friend to buy a variety of fish and shellfish.

The visit was his third to Scarborough to buy seafood at Ocean's Pantry, which he told staff was the best and freshest place to get fish in Britain.

Coun Don Robinson said: 'His visit is good for the harbour, good for trade and good for Scarborough.

The harbour is increasingly becoming a tourist attraction in its own right and Ocean's Pantry is a jewel in the crown of the fishing pier.

The shop is so hygienic, so modern and you can see the fish being filleted.'

Mr Jason and his friend bought halibut steak, plaice and a crab from the crab stalls.'

## 2011

A battalion of volunteers is being sought to help the organisers of this year's Scarborough Armed Forces Day.

More than 10,000 people are expected to gather on the Foreshore for the town's third Armed Forces Day on Saturday, June 25.

In the run up to the event organisers are looking for volunteers to help with a variety of tasks, including collecting for the three charities supported by this year's Armed Forces Day – the Royal British Legion, Soldiers, Sailors, Airmen and Families Association (SSAFA), Forces Help and the RNLI – as well as stewarding and marshalling duties.

Among the attractions planned for Armed Forces Day are an aeronautical display by the Blades team, a 15 minute display of the Battle of Britain Memorial Flight Lancaster Bomber, marching bands, a veterans' parade and stalls, events and activities.

This year's event is being hosted and organised by Scarborough Council, in partnership with the Heroes Welcome initiative, South Bay Traders Association, Royal British Legion, SSAFA Forces Help and the RNLI, with financial support from local businessman Don Robinson, the Ministry of Defence and the council.

## 2012 - Four men to be made a Freeman of the town.

Eminent Scarborough residents are set to be officially honoured as freemen of the borough.

Former boxing world champion Paul Ingle and ex-Scarborough Football Club chairman Don Robinson will be bestowed with the Freedom of the Borough of Scarborough during a special ceremony.

Andrew and Tim Boyes, who have helped shape the success of their Scarborough-based business empire, will also receive the accolade.

And former Scarborough mayor and councillor Lucy Haycock will be made an Honorary Alderman for services given to the council between 1983 and 2011.

The honour has only been given to 15 people since Scarborough Council was given the power to make the award in 1974.

Previous recipients include Sir Alan Ayckbourn.

Scarborough Council is set to host a lavish ceremony at the Town Hall on Tuesday, April 17th, to honour the quintet.

During the service in the Council Chamber, Scarborough mayor Cllr John Blackburn will invite each individual to sign the Freemen's Roll before presenting them with a sealed copy of the Resolution.

Edgehill fighter Ingle, 39, who rose through the ranks to become IBF featherweight champion before being forced to retire after a bout in December 2000, said he was overwhelmed by the award.

He added: 'I'm absolutely chuffed. If it wasn't for the support of the people of Scarborough I would never have achieved what I did. I would like to thank everyone in the borough who has supported me.'

His accolade will be put forward by Cllr Tom Fox and seconded by Cllr Bill Chatt.

Mr Robinson, 77, who is a previous president of Scarborough Cricket Club, will see his Freeman title backed by Cllr Peter Popple and Cllr David Jeffels.

Mr Robinson added he was 'thunderstruck' at his appointment.

Andrew Boyes said he was delighted to receive the honour alongside his cousin Tim.

Together the pair have been at the helm of the Boyes empire for more than four decades as joint managing directors.

Andrew, who is now chairman of the company, said: 'As a Scarborough guy, born and bred, to be recognised like this is fantastic and a huge honour.

'I could not think of anything I would rather have. It is fantastic too to be recognised alongside Tim as we have been somewhat of a double act all this time.'

Cllr David Billing and Cllr John Ritchie will move and second his Resolution, with Cllr Derek Bastiman and Cllr

Jane Kenyon backing Tim's standing as a Borough Freeman.

The ceremony will then honour Mrs Haycock, with Cllr Tom Fox proposing the title of Honorary Alderman and Cllr David Jeffels seconding it.

She added: 'For some people to become the mayor, they say it is the icing on the cake. I was not expecting that so to get this title is the cherry on top of that. It is most humbling and I am very grateful for it.'

# CHAPTER 8

## 1974   - The Royal Opera House years
## 1979   - The Coronia

*Photo 1990 courtesy Fred Bottle*

Don Robinson recalls, 'I had a company called Millett Investors Limited which had originally been incorporated as an investment company to cover my private interests. However, the company acquired The Royal Opera House, Scarborough, in 1974 from the York Repertory Company.

We then let the theatre to a trust that had previously been formed by the Scarborough people to prevent the theatre's closure. It was operated unsuccessfully by the trust for approximately 2 years; no rent was paid to us and the theatre was left empty.

We had to take the theatre back and we modernised it with a new roof, chandeliers, new stage lighting and new bars and we reopened it, and for 12 years it did very well.

For example, Ken Dodd did two shows nightly for a two or three year period and other top artists including Norman Wisdom topped the bill through the years. We had Junior Showtime in the morning, cinema in the afternoon, good variety artists in the evening and midnight hypnotist shows. We had two bars open to the public – so we were open morning noon and night, seven days a week.

Then it was bought from my Company by the Jay family from Great Yarmouth around 1988 for £350,000. They operated summer theatres. Their main interests were at Great Yarmouth and also in other resorts'.

A later press cutting from the Scarborough Evening News reported:

'1992 - The Royal Opera House, with its two bars and Rosie's fun pub, was being put up for sale, impresario Peter Jay said this week.

He had bought the place only four years before for £350,000.

Mr Jay – who was a pop star in the 1960s with Peter Jay and the Jaywalkers – said he was selling because of the pressure of business commitments elsewhere.

He and the Royal Opera House Theatre Club urged the Borough Council to buy the Victorian building and turn it into a civic theatre.

Mr Jay had originally intended to develop the Opera House as a cabaret-style venue with dancing and dining. He shelved this plan after a disappointing summer season in 1988, and then the theatre reverted to being a full-time cinema.

Mr Jay bought the complex from entertainments giant Kunick, of which Scarborough businessman Don Robinson was then deputy chairman.

It was Mr Robinson who saved the Opera House from demolition in 1976 when he bought it and restored it to become a leading seaside theatre.

Mr Jay was not able to sell and eventually receivers took over the building.

*

When the photograph on the next page was taken the theatre was already 130 years old. An article published in 1901 in The Playgoer and accompanying the photograph says,

'Few theatres existing can boast so historic and dramatic record as the Theatre Royal, Scarborough. The Rev. Thomas Haggitt, a clergyman of the Church of England, built it just one hundred and thirty years ago for Thomas Bates, a celebrated comedian of the day, who controlled it for about forty years, when it was purchased by Stephen Kemble (brother of Mrs. Siddons), since which time nearly every popular actor and actress have appeared on its boards.

The house is now owned by Mrs. Henry Mayhew, who has in Mr FP Morgan a capable, courteous, and most enterprising manager.'

*The Theatre Royal built in 1771 photographed in 1901*

# Theatre Royal, Scarboro'.

PROPRIETOR AND MANAGER............MR. ROXBY

## GREAT ATTRACTION!

First Time this season, Sheridan's celebrated Play of

# PIZARRO!

And First Time of the highly popular GHOST STORY, of the

## CORSICAN BROTHERS AS AN AFTERPIECE.

## Market Night.

This present THURSDAY, July 23rd, 1857,

Will be presented, the grand Tragic Play called

# PIZARRO;

## OR, SPANIARDS IN PERU.

### PERUVIANS.

| | | |
|---|---|---|
| Atalila, King of Quito | Mr. H. LANGTON | |
| Orozimbo | Mr. BENSON—Peruvian Boy | Mr. W. J. EVANS—Orozembo | Mr. C. H. SIMMS |
| High Priest | Mr. BLYDE—Cora | Miss R. CRANE—Almand's Child | Miss CATTLE |
| Priestesses and Virgins of the Sun | Miss C. H. SIMMS, Mrs F. HASTINGS, Mrs J. CONWAY—Blind Man | Mrs E. CAMERON |
| | Mrs J. TYRRELL, Miss L CRANE, Mrs M. W. HOLLAND, &c. | Miss MURRAY |

### SPANIARDS.

| | | |
|---|---|---|
| Pizarro | Mr. CHARLES COOKE | |
| Almagro | Mr. W. HOLLAND—Davilla | Mr. STERNE |
| Elvira | Mr. FREDERICK HASTINGS—Sentinel | Mr. JOHN NEWTON—Antonio | Miss ELY LOVEDAY |

The whole to conclude with, the most successful Drama ever produced in Scarborough, called THE

# CORSICAN BROTHERS:

## OR, THE COMPACT OF DEATH.

| | | |
|---|---|---|
| Mons. Fabien del Franchi | | |
| Mons. Louis del Franchi | Twin Brothers of Corsica | |
| Mons. de Chateau Renaud | Mr. W. J. EVANS |
| Mons. alfred Meynard, a Friend of Louis del Franchi | Mr. FREDERICK HASTINGS |
| Le Baron de Montgiron | Mr. W. J. EVANS |
| Orlando | The Heads of Two Corsican Families, Le Baron thirst three Martelli, between whom the Vendetta | Mr. G. F. DE VERE |
| Colimena | or deadly feud is established whose the Vendetta | Mr. W. HOLLAND |
| Mons. Verner | | Mr. J. TYRRELL |
| Antonio Sabini, Judge of the District | Mr. STERNE—Griffo, a domestic of Madame del Franchi | Mr. C. H. SIMMS |
| Baptiste, a Woodcutter | Mr. JOHN NEWTON—Surveo Fierro | Mr. BLYDE |
| Madame Savilia del Franchi, Mother of the Corsican Brothers | Mr. E. CAMERON |
| Coralie Vitempe, Leopartre | Miss ELY LOVEDAY |
| Celestine de L'Estrange | Mrs F. HASTINGS |
| Emilie de Lesparre | Mrs J. CONWAY |
| Estelle Fernandez | Dancers at the Grand Opera | Miss L CRANE |
| Marie | | Mrs J. TYRRELL |

### Act 1.

**Hall in the Chateau of Madame Sevilla del Franchi.**
The strange Guest—History of the Corsican Superstition—the
Brothers—the Warning—the Supernatural Appearance.

## THE VISION OF THE DUEL.

### Act 2.

**Interior of Box Lobby of the Opera House, Paris**
During a Masquerade Ball and Carnival—
The Roue and his Victim—the Invitation to Supper—THE WAGER—
**Scene 2.—Mansion of Mons. le Baron de Montgiron**
THE EXPOSURE—THE CHALLENGE—
**Scene 3rd.—Glade in the Forest of Fontainbleau—Winter—**
(The Incidents of the First Act in Corsica, and the Second Act in Paris, are supposed to occur at the same time.)

### Act 3.

**The Clearing in the Forest of Fontainbleau.**
The scene of the Fatal Duel....the Woodcutter....the accident....extraordinary warning to Chateau Renaud....the
terrible meeting....the terrible and deadly conflict....retributive justice....with impressive and

## Supernatural Denouement and TABLEAU.

The Box Office of the Theatre will be open on each day of Performance, from Eleven till One, and from Two
till Four, under the management of Mr. Gilbert, where Tickets and Places for the Boxes may be secured.

**Doors open at Seven o'clock, and the Performance to commence as HALF-PAST SEVEN precisely.**

SECOND PRICE will be taken at the commencement of the afterpiece, as near Nine o'Clock as possible.

| | | |
|---|---|---|
| **Boxes 3s.** | **Pit 2s.** | **Gallery 1s.** |
| **Boxes 2s.** | **Pit 1s.** | **Gallery 6d.** |

Manager, Mr. S. Roxby, 29, St. Nicholas' Street.—Stage Manager, Mr. Harry Beverly.

FIRST PROMA.

C., & S. TODD, PRINTERS, 14, KING STREET, SCARBOROUGH.

## The following extract from The Theatres' Trust describes the Royal Opera House in detail:

'The demolition of the Royal Opera House was one of the most regrettable and avoidable theatrical losses of recent years following, as it did, on the destruction in 1999 of the interior of Scarborough's early music hall, the Alexandra. The levelling of the Opera House occurred at a time when the general trend throughout the country was one of celebration at the restoration and triumphant reopening of theatres and it occurred in a place that should have been particularly alive to its theatrical heritage. Scarborough had an active theatre in the eighteenth century.

It was a great entertainment resort in the nineteenth century and is now home to the Stephen Joseph Theatre whose formative artistic director (1972-2009) was the distinguished playwright, [Sir] Alan Ayckbourn.

In 1998 the building was flooded and rotting, the result of neglect and vandalism compounded by a lack of action by authorities regarding the fate of the listed building.

*

The description that follows was written in 1998 and is reproduced unamended. The building had a short-lived predecessor, as Charles Adnams Grand Circus, a wooden building, which opened in 1876. It was rebuilt the following year as a brick structure designed by John Petch. This building lasted as a circus and music hall until February 1908 when it was demolished apart from the outer walls and a series of cast iron columns. Local architect Frank Tugwell (architect of the Futurist Theatre) designed the present theatre which opened in 1908. The foyer block is separate from the auditorium and possibly of a different date and may originally have been a terrace of three houses. The left hand one forms the foyer which links through to the auditorium; above are flats. The auditorium is on three levels, seating 970. The layout of the three boxes either side of the proscenium is most unusual with two at dress circle level and the major one suspended above the stalls. The circle is high above the stalls giving unusually good sightlines from the rear stalls. There are twenty-one rows of seats in the stalls, seven in the dress circle and three in the balcony which has been reduced in size. The circle has a horseshoe form with a restrained scroll and tasselled decoration. The balcony is serpentine in shape with straight slips returned to the proscenium wall. The proscenium is segmentally arched and richly decorated with scrolls, groups of cherubs and a central cartouche containing horses' heads, recalling the early circus use and Hippodrome name. The circles are partly cantilevered with one supporting pillar at stalls and circle levels. Sightlines are excellent throughout. The ceiling is plain and simply panelled. This must now be one of the most important 'sleeping beauties' in the country and is crying out for restoration and reopening, especially with the planned demise of the Futurist. However the auditorium is now flooded, the foyer block ruined after a series of arson attacks and action is urgently needed to halt the rot.'

## The Scarborough News reported on the opening of the Royal Opera House Casino:

'The new Scarborough Opera House Casino has been heralded as the most important new development in decades.

The £7m development on the site of the former Royal Opera House site opened last night.

Workers toiled around the clock to make sure the state-of-the-art casino was ready for the opening.

Two years ago the old theatre was covered in scaffolding, the roof had collapsed and the inside was under 8ft of water. Guests praised Nikolas and Rebecca Shaw, of Nikolas Shaw, the company behind the venture.

Scarborough businessman Don Robinson said: 'This is the best thing to happen in Scarborough for the past 25 years. This is a great boost for all the hotels and guest houses and I hope that with The Sands North Bay development this is the start for a new Scarborough.

This is as good as Las Vegas.'

Scarborough businessman Malcolm Stephenson, former owner of The Crown Hotel and Marvels, said: 'This is Scarborough going in the right direction. Private investment is what Scarborough always needed and full credit to the Shaws.'

Graham North, chairman of the Forum for Tourism, said: 'This is what Scarborough really needs – something new and different. This will help the conference trade and is something the town should be proud of. There are only eight places like this in the UK and Scarborough has one of them."

Money was raised on the night for St Catherine's Hospice.'

## 1979 - The Coronia

In 1979 Millet Investors Limited, Don Robinson's company which had originally bought the Royal Opera House, acquired the Coronia, a pleasure steamer then operating from Scarborough. In 1981 Millet also developed the Showboat Bar adjoining the Royal Opera House. The Coronia was run successfully until 1985 when Don sold it to his manager and friend Tommy Hanson; but not for use in Scarborough. Instead, she headed south to Gibraltar where she ran for six years, on short cruises around the rock and to see the dolphins.

A Dolphin Centre was opened in Gibraltar and Steve Walton, whom Don holds in very high regard, was dolphin trainer, a role he originally held at Flamingo Park. Don's eldest son Nicky also went out to Gibraltar to gain business experience

*MV Coronia, Scarborough*

In 1991 Tom Machin, of North Sea Leisure, bought the Coronia and brought her back from Gibraltar to join her previous fleet mate Regal Lady which, by then was back in Scarborough.

In late 2010 the Coronia's future in Scarborough was under threat and Scarborough and Whitby MP, Robert Goodwill, rescued the ship for Scarborough by purchasing it and leasing it back to operator, Tom Machin. She now carries out her historic duties alongside her sister ship, Regal Lady.

*

Millet also owned various investment properties and, in 1982, bought a 50% interest in the Scene 1 and Scene 2 discotheques located on the corner of Aberdeen Walk in Scarborough.

In 1983 the whole of the Millet share capital was sold to Kunick Holdings Plc for cash and shares. This valued the company at £720,000. In the same year Don was appointed vice-chairman of Kunick plc.

# CHAPTER 9

# THE FOOTBALL YEARS

Don Robinson made his first trip to the Athletic Ground where 'boro played in Scarborough when he was about 10 years old.

'When I was 13, I scored the winning goal for Friarage school at the 'boro ground,' Robinson said. 'We beat Gladstone Road 2-1 so my association with 'boro goes back 67 years at least.'

Robinson says he was asked to become a director of the club in the late 60s by Tommy Stephenson, then managing director of Plaxton Coach Builders and Chairman of Scarborough FC. In 1974 Don was first appointed Chairman before stepping down to make way for John Fawcett a year later. However, he remained a director and in February 1977 was appointed chairman for the second time – this time when the club's reputation had improved but its debts had risen to £150,000.

He says: 'I was so proud and honoured to be asked. I became chairman of the club at a time when Scarborough was considered to be the best non-league side in the country.'

In 1972 Robinson even approached footballing superstar George Best to come and play for the club after the Manchester United ace announced he wouldn't mind playing for a non-league side. 'I spoke to him on the phone and he agreed to come and talk to us, but problems with his contract meant the deal fell through.'

Scarborough resident Andrew Jenkinson remembers Best's visit to Scarborough in the 1980s when he attended Crystals Garage Quiz Night.

He said: "He was everything any man would aspire to be – he was good looking, could pull the girls, could play football and liked a beer. I am a Manchester United fan and think he was one of the best players ever.

'I once had a football that had been signed by Best, Charlton and Law, but my children found it and thought it was just another ball to play with. They took it out and played with it in the street and ruined it. I don't think I told them off – I think I just broke down and cried.'

Robinson remembers the times when the 'boro players would take part in the Scarborough Carnival parade.

He said: 'We were part of a community and the town was proud of its football team.

I remember the open top bus tour when we had won the FA Trophy at Wembley. The town was packed and roads were blocked with cars. So many people wanted to see us. There were one or two players with tears in their eyes, it was so emotional.'

'We ran the club as a business and always kept a tight control of the finances, getting rid of the debt. In fact one year we finished the season with £200,000 in the bank. I remained as chairman until September 1982 – that was over 10 years with Scarborough.

In March 1982 I was approached by the Needler family to take over at Hull City. I agreed and at that time Scarborough had built up net assets of £400,000 and was held up as an example of how a football club business should be run."

I was therefore running both clubs but the pressure began to tell and in September 1982 I resigned from Scarborough.

\*

The first ever time Scarborough FC played an association football match was on 6 November 1880 at the

*'Boro chairman Don Robinson carries manager Colin Appleton after the Cup presentation*

Cricket Ground against Bridlington. Scarborough won the game 2–1. Almost 100 years later when the club was in difficulties Don Robinson became chairman and with his zest and business acumen turned a loss making enterprise into a profitable and successful club.

During his 10 year tenure non-league football was revolutionised with the creation of the Alliance Premier League just below the Football League. This took effect from the start of the 1980s. With Robinson as chairman, Scarborough was able to improve many elements of its ground to enable it to meet more rigorous requirements and the club entered the new league.

1972—73 was particularly notable all round with Colin Appleton at the helm as manager. The club finished as runners-up in the league, missing out on the top spot to Boston United. The same season Scarborough knocked Oldham Athletic out of the FA Cup, before going out to Doncaster Rovers once again in the Second Round. In the FA Trophy the club earned a trip to Wembley where they defeated Wigan Athletic 2—1. For the rest of the decade Scarborough managed to finish in the top 5 within the league, but it was their cup runs which gained wide attention.

Boro' made it to Wembley in the FA Trophy for four finals during the mid-1970s; in 1973 they beat Wigan Athletic 2-1; in 1975 they lost 4—0 to Matlock Town; in 1976 they beat Stafford Rangers 3—2 with Sean Marshall grabbing the winning goal in extra time; and in 1977 they played against Dagenham.

The late John Barnes was Chairman in 'Wembley' year 1973, John Fawcett in 1976 and Don was Chairman in the other two 'Wembley' years 1975 and 1977.

Little did Don Robinson know at that time that one day in the future he would almost become the largest shareholder in Wembley Stadium.

In the FA Cup the Seasiders had two significant runs in the latter part of the 1970s which saw them reach the Third Round. First in 1975—76, Scarborough knocked out Preston North End, before losing 2—1 to eventual semi-finalists Crystal Palace in a game screened on *Match of the Day*. Again in 1977—78, Scarborough reached the Third Round before losing to Brighton & Hove Albion. The club celebrated its centenary year in 1979.

Non-league football was revolutionised with the creation of the Alliance Premier League just below the Football League for the start of the 1980s. With Don Robinson as chairman, and keeping tight control of finances, Scarborough was able to improve many elements of its ground which enabled it to enter the new league.

After building up a squad with seasoned former Football League players in 1980-81, Scarborough mounted a decent challenge for the championship but eventually finished third. Colin Williams was a key player for Scarborough during this time, finishing as Alliance Premier League top scorer for two seasons in a row.

But in 1982 Robinson was head hunted by the Needler family to take over Hull City which was in severe financial trouble in the hands of the receivers.

Whilst he agreed to move to Hull, to a city for which he still has great affection, and became chairman of Hull City Football Club in 1982, there was an overlap of 6 months before he resigned as Scarborough's chairman. He was chairman of Hull for 7 years. Again, hard graft and logical business decisions linked by his common sense and his love of sport turned the club from insolvency into a profitable enterprise for each of the years he was involved.

In August 2010 former Scarborough and York footballer Ken Boyes passed away aged 75. The former captain of Scarborough, who later managed the club in

1973-74, was highly regarded as one of the best players ever to play for the club.

Boyes also sealed success for the club at Wembley in the 1970s, something former Scarborough Chairman Don Robinson remembers fondly.

Robinson said: "Since I have been working within football in Scarborough, the best three local lads who I've seen play for the club were Tony Aveyard, who died after a match at the Athletic Ground, Colin Appleton, and Ken.

'Ken was Scarborough through and through and the town should be proud of him and what he achieved with the club.

'When we won the FA Trophy at Wembley I remember the open topped bus tour round Scarborough where he wouldn't let go of the trophy all the way back to the Royal Hotel. That's how much the town and the club meant to him.'

\*\*\*

## HULL CITY FOOTBALL CLUB

'The best years of my life: Don Robinson recalls his Hull City takeover.

Philip Buckingham of the Hull Daily Mail met Don Robinson in 2012:

'To mark the 30th anniversary of Don Robinson's unveiling as Hull City chairman, I met up with the colourful former *chief to recall how he first took over the cash-strapped Tigers in May 1982.'*

'Even at the grand old age of 78, Don Robinson still has a sparkle in the eye at the very mention of Hull City.

'Of all the things I've done, and I've certainly done a few, those were the best years of my life,' he says.

City supporters of a certain vintage can certainly empathise.

If Robinson was the artist behind one of Boothferry Park's most colourful periods, this week marks the 30th anniversary of his very first brush-stroke.

Engaging and enthusiastic, he was the Tigers' irrepressible showman for almost a decade in East Yorkshire.

Overseeing a climb from the depths of receivership to the brink of the top flight Robinson almost single-handedly found a heartbeat on East Yorkshire's sleeping giant during an unforgettable journey as chairman. And he did so in style.

As he reflects on a landmark anniversary in City's history, Robinson finds two causes for minor regret in his reservoir of happy thoughts. One is that he could not be the man to first inspire top-flight football for the Tigers. The other is that City are still to play on the moon. The memories of a magical reign may have blurred at the edges as Robinson enjoys retirement from his Scarborough home, but his trademark eccentricity shows little sign of fading. "Why shouldn't we want to be the first team on the moon?" he asks with a broad grin, recalling his famed ambition first dreamed up ahead of City's Anglo-American Cup clash with Tampa Bay Rowdies in 1984.

'If we ever do get that far, I'd still like to play centre forward.'

You suspect his wife of 56 years, Jean, has heard it all before. Almost apologetically she rolls her eyes.

The couple have lived in the same cliff-top house overlooking Scarborough's North Bay for over 40 years and Jean perhaps offered up a similar response when plans to bail out an ailing Division Four club were coming to fruition 30 years ago.

Unable to stem spiralling debts, [£500,000 for the 1981/2 season] chairman Christopher Needler had taken drastic action by calling in the receivers to Boothferry Park on February 25th, 1982.

*The Holiday Inn Tampa Bay, welcome the Hull team*

*Above: Tampa Bay Rowdies team in the Anglo-American cup*
*Below: The Hull City team in bowler hats and with umbrellas in Disney World, Florida*

City had become the first Football League team plunged into such a mess and although a bright end to the season had defied a darkening mood, the club's viability remained in question.

It was then that Robinson was the subject of a desperate SOS.

Having earned a sound reputation in building up non-league Scarborough over a 10 year period, Robinson was invited to perform similar miracles with the Tigers.'

'I got the shock of my life when I got a call from Christopher Needler's finance director to see if I would get involved,' recalls Robinson.

'I thought they were joking at first when they asked me to come and run it. In later life you begin to realise why and that was because we'd done such a good job with making Scarborough so financially sound, but it had come as a big surprise.'

Robinson's time in charge of Scarborough had brought two FA Trophy successes in 1976 and 1977, and transformed the Seasiders into non-league football's richest club.

City was an altogether different proposition. Relegation to Division Four for the first time in 1980-81 had the Tigers on their knees and deep in the red. Robinson was the financial nurse, but the next step could well have been a priest.

'You always looked at Hull City and Boothferry Park and to me that was like Wembley,' Robinson added.

'I used to think as a kid 'Wow, Boothferry Park' because it was such a great ground. Hull City were like sleeping giants.'

It was that allure that convinced Robinson to take a giant leap of faith on May 15, 1982.

Ending the 1981-82 season in receivership marked City's darkest hour but the dawn would break 24 hours after a final day 2-2 draw at Halifax Town.

Three months of uncertainty had followed the Tigers' inglorious February demise, with question marks even hanging over City's Football League existence.

Then, to the rescue, rode Robinson. Striking a complex deal with outgoing chairman Needler, Robinson paid £250,000 to become the majority shareholder, while Boothferry Park was purchased by a "recreational foundation" set up by the Needler family to safeguard the long-term future of City's home.

Overdue security was finally forthcoming and Robinson was the proud owner of a Football League club. A cause for celebration and a deep breath, as he recalls.

'My first thought when I got in and looked through the books was 'What on earth have I done?' but once you do something like that you've got to make it work.

You can't walk away, you've got to see it through. The first thing we did was to form a board where everyone could be part of a team but we were very hands on.

'We'd sell raffle tickets when fans were coming into the ground and we'd meet them on the train platform.

I'd be there on a match day shouting 'Get your raffle tickets, help Hull City' but that was all part of turning the club around. We'd have done anything.'

Robinson arrived at Boothferry Park with all the colour and zeal to light up a monochrome landscape.

Although born in Batley, a childhood in Scarborough had set him out on a quite unique path through life.

As well as boxing at the Royal Albert Hall and time spent as a pro' wrestler, Robinson also had a short career with Hull KR between 1957 and 1960.

'I wasn't very good,' he says, but that spell with Rovers made the first real introductions to East Yorkshire.

After building up his fortune through a variety of forays into the leisure industry, at 48 he walked into the boardroom at Boothferry Park to begin breathing life back into City.

Robinson's first step was to recruit Colin Appleton, his trusted boss at Scarborough, and inheriting a young side flush with potential, the returns for the Midas pair were instant.

Losing just six games in the 1982-83 season, City finished runners-up to Wimbledon to claw back into the third tier at the second time of asking.

Supporters, tired of the drip, drip, drip of previous failures, were rejuvenated. A year after crowds at Boothferry Park had fallen as low as 3,040, as many as 14,410 had turned up to see the Tigers canter to promotion. Among them was Robinson, who had insisted on buying his season ticket during a bid to encourage sales.

'The biggest thing in football and in Hull is the fans,' he said. 'It's their club, always will be, no one else's. I felt I was part of those fans and I wanted to win as much as any fan.'

*Don with [now Sir] Elton John at Hull City. He bought Don a crate of champagne*

That spirit lives on in Robinson as he enjoys the quiet life back in Scarborough but 30 years ago he was responsible for guiding City out of the dark and into the light. And the journey was only just beginning.

Promotion to Division Three followed in 1983, (photo above) with a young team featuring the likes of future England international Brian Marwood, future England manager Steve McClaren, centre-forward Billy Whitehurst, and the prolific goal-scorer Les Mutrie. When Hull City missed out on promotion by one goal the following season, Appleton left to manage Swansea City and after 7 years chairing the Hull City Board Don resigned.

He continues to keep an eye on the fortunes of the Tigers from his home in Scarborough and has watched with interest the restoration job undertaken by present owners Assem and Ehab Allam.

Just as he saved City at Boothferry Park, the Allams pulled the Tigers back from the brink in December 2010.

The decision to axe Nick Barmby has invited the first criticism upon their reign from some quarters, but Robinson believes the City board took the right decision.

'Just at the moment football is suffering from people who are only interested in making quick money,' he said.

'I'm pleased to see that's not happening with Hull City and what's been done by the Allams is fantastic.

'The first thing they had to do was to run it on a firm financial footing. If they run it as a business for the community, it'll be the best thing that's happened there.

'I'm very sorry for young Nick Barmby but you can't have your manager saying 'spend, spend, spend.'

*Left: Assem Allam*

'This thing happens in football all the time now. A manager is there to manage, leave the financial control to the board and the chairman.'

While the stakes have changed along with the times, Robinson's sound business acumen continues to demand respect.

After guiding Scarborough out of financial trouble between 1977 and 1982, he repeated the trick with the Tigers during a seven-year stint as chairman.

'Any football club should be at the heart of a community and some of the modern clubs don't realise that,' he added.

'When we went into Scarborough it was in the red, it was bankrupt, but we put in a little bit of money through a loan and within two years we had it in the black.

'All we ever did for ground improvements was out of our own money, we never borrowed from banks.

We'd also done a lot to get the town together and brought in people who weren't football fanatics. That is what every club should always look to do rather than spending money they haven't got.'

*

However, all was not plain sailing as described by Eddie Gray in his book Eddie Gray – *Marching on Together.*

[Eddie Gray took over at Hull City for the 1988–89 season following the departure of Brian Horton the previous season. Hull managed to pull into mid-table and only five points short of the play-offs in February, and they reached the FA Cup fifth round where they lost to Liverpool. Only 1 win in the last 18 games meant that Hull finished fourth from bottom, yet clear of relegation danger, but the poor form led to his departure.]

'Hull had been on the slide before I arrived. They were third in the Second Division in 1985, and over the next three seasons finished sixth, fourteenth and fifteenth. In my season as manager, 1988-89, it was twenty-first (which, being the same spot that Rochdale had filled in my two seasons there, raised the tongue-in-cheek comment among my friends that at least I was consistent). As I anticipated, the Hull slide continued after I left.

One reason why I did not enjoy this job was my relationship with Hull's extrovert chairman and owner, Don Robinson. There was a clash of personalities, which was accentuated by the fact that I was in much closer contact with Robinson than I had been with Tommy Cannon at Rochdale. Robinson wanted me to move to Hull but I kept putting it off. The longer we worked together, the more I realised that our association was not going to work.

There was a lot to admire about Don Robinson. A

former wrestler, boxer and rugby league player, he was an entrepreneur with a capital E. Before taking over at Hull in 1982, he had been chairman of Scarborough, and laid the foundations for the club's entry into the Football League. At Hull, he took the club out of receivership, and steered them from the Fourth Division to the Second in his first two seasons. As a figure with an acute sense of showmanship, he became even more famous for publicity gimmicks such as riding a horse around the pitch dressed in a rodeo outfit, and bringing a tame brown bear into the club. It was typical of him that when Hull played Liverpool at home in the FA Cup fifth round in the season I was there, one part of the ground was adorned with a banner which drew attention to the physical approach of our centre-forward Billy Whitehurst, and proclaimed, 'Go get 'em, Rambo'

The Messiah of Boothferry Park he might have been, but I found him overpowering, particularly in relation to the areas of the club that I felt were my responsibility. One point of conflict between us concerned the short mid-season break he organised for the players in Bermuda. I was invited to go, too, but I felt that it would be better to remain at home and concentrate on trying to find players who could strengthen the side. That decision turned out to be a mistake because when they got back, I was amazed to learn that Robinson had taken it upon himself to give them his own training sessions and that much of their work involved running up and down sand dunes. That was the last thing they needed as far as I was concerned — it was the sort of training players did in the close season, when building up their fitness after the summer break. But when I challenged Robinson about this, he explained that he felt they needed 'toughening up'.

I also found it difficult to accept his pre-match dressing-room visits to give the players the benefit of his advice — advice that in a number of cases, I did not agree with.

Robinson typified the new breed of football club chairmen in England; men for whom football is a business, not a hobby, and who adopt much more of a hands-on approach than their counterparts in the past. The urge to pull all the strings at Hull was one that Robinson appeared to me to find difficult to resist. I admired his drive, but as far as I was concerned, the way it was applied did not make him an easy person to work for. In common with a lot of chairmen, I think Robinson made the mistake of assuming that the principles that had made his other businesses successful were bound to work in football, too. Because of the many and varied imponderables involved, football is unique.

For someone like Robinson, Hull's results after they reached the Second Division will have been very hard to take. The fact that I could not stop the slide was disappointing for me, too, especially as we had a tremendous pair of strikers in Keith Edwards and Billy Whitehurst. Keith, a quiet, unassuming person who had played for Leeds under Billy Bremner, was one of the best finishers I have worked with. I felt he was not assertive enough at times, but his scoring record that season meant that I could never be too dogmatic about this. Then in his second spell at Hull, he was the Second Division's top scorer with 26 league goals and an overall total of 30.

Lack of assertiveness was never a problem for Billy Whitehurst, who I signed from Sunderland and who was the perfect foil for Keith. Billy, 6ft tall and weighing 13 stone, was the strongest and most intimidating centre-forward I have worked with. He became a cult figure at Hull, as he did at his other clubs, because he made the likes of Joe Jordan and Mark Hughes seem almost genteel. Players really were scared of him. Not long ago, I was discussing Billy with Leeds' goalkeeper Nigel Martyn, who recounted a match he played against him for Crystal Palace. There was a clash between the two and Nigel, showing his recklessness in those days, tried to out-psyche him. 'I will see you after the game,' he said. Later, when Nigel was having a drink with his centre-half Andy Thorn in the players' lounge, he felt a tap on his shoulder. He turned around and there was Billy glaring at him. 'You still want to have a go then?' Billy asked him. Nigel recalled that Thorn and everybody else in close proximity to him suddenly disappeared. Needless to say, his reply to Billy was not in the affirmative.

Billy was happy to fight anyone, and from what I heard he was not too bothered about how many were against him. He knew no fear. On a couple of occasions, he would come in for training with bruises and cuts on his face, which always caused me to wonder what the other fellow (or fellows) must have looked like.

Although Billy was a very strong-minded character, I got on well with him. I knew how to handle him and he never gave me any trouble. Apart from being good in the air, his touch was not bad for someone of his build. He did a good job for me.

Not long after my sacking at the end of that season, I was surprised to get a call from him at my home on a Sunday morning. He had become the most influential member of the squad, and he put it to me that he could use this to get me back to the club. 'All the boys want you back, Eddie,' he said. 'I will lead a deputation to the chairman.' I appreciated the thought, but even if Don Robinson had changed his mind, there is no way I could have gone back..."

Don says he disagrees with many assertions made in Eddie Gray's above extract. But with tongue firmly in cheek Don says, "He was and is a nice guy. But when he was Manager if he'd picked me for the team we'd have won every match and I'd even have played for nothing!

*

On 20th March 1990 and towards the end of Don's very successful reign at Hull City, The Malton branch of Barclays Bank became Hull City's Ball sponsor for the evening. The match was against Stoke and a group of 10 staff and bank clients (one a Stoke supporter!) arrived in a mini bus for the City v Stoke match. The score was 0-0 and the attendance 6,456.

# CHAPTER 10

## 1983 - The Kunick Years

The Kunick Group of which Don Robinson was Deputy Chairman was founded in 1983 and covered a wide spectrum of business activities, from tourist attractions such as the London, York and Paris Dungeons, to gaming machines in 9,000 venues nationwide.

The company had been a dormant clothing trade concern when Don and the former holiday camp tycoon, Sir Fred Pontin, took a further step towards creating a substantial new leisure group by agreeing to take over Scarborough Zoo and Marineland.

The Scarborough business, originally started by Don, was being acquired from Trident Television through National Leisure Group, a new company being formed by Don and Sir Fred from the shell of the former Kunick Holdings.

Don Robinson, the Hull City Football Club chairman at the time, and Sir Fred moved in on Kunick early in 1983 when they injected their existing leisure interests into the company in return for shares and cash.

Further acquisitions were already being considered at Kunick, where the authorised share capital was being doubled to £10m. In its new guise, the company intended to apply for a relisting of its shares on the Stock Exchange later in the year.

Trident received just over 3m. Kunick shares in return for its Scarborough business, giving it 21.5 per cent of the enlarged share capital of the new leisure vehicle.

As a result of the share issue, the interest of Don Robinson and his associates was reduced to 42.4 per cent, compared with the 57 per cent acquired earlier in 1983 when he injected his own Scarborough leisure businesses into Kunick.

Don had the largest shareholding in Kunick in 1996 with 2,891,350 shares – down from 3,140,000 in 1985 following Trident's involvement.

Sir Fred, who injected the Farringford Hotel, Freshwater, Isle of Wight, into Kunick earlier this year [1983] saw his interest reduced in view of the increased share capital.

The Scarborough business which was acquired from Trident comprised an amusement park, and Zoo and Marineland on a 6 acre site near the seafront.

It was started by Don Robinson in the mid-1960s. Trident acquired full control in 1977 and Don was managing director since the business started including during Trident's tenure.

In a separate deal, Kunick also agreed to acquire the 50 per cent interest that it does not already own in Scarborough Scene One and Scene discotheques'.

The Times 1st, September 1983 reported:

'At an age when most people settle for comfortable retirement Sir Fred Pontin, the former holiday camp tycoon, is preparing for a stock market comeback and, as a sideline developing a West Country hotel chain.

At the Grosvenor Hotel in London yesterday, he presided at a shareholders meeting of Kunick Holdings, fashion group that fell on hard times and now, as a leisure business, is the vehicle for Sir Fred's stock market return. After the meeting he travelled to Brixham, Devon, to complete his latest hotel purchase.

Sir Fred, who will be 77 next month, is, at least for the time being, keeping his two business careers apart.

Kunick Holdings, which is to be renamed the National

Leisure Group, has more than 600 shareholders. Just six of them turned up yesterday to vote through the latest acquisition, the takeover of Scarborough Zoo and Marineland, an amusement centre at the Yorkshire resort.

Since Sir Fred joined forces earlier this year with Donald Robinson, [then] aged 46, Kunick has made a series of acquisitions. These include an Isle of Wight hotel, sold by Sir Fred, and various leisure interests in Scarborough acquired largely from Mr Robinson.

Sir Fred told the six shareholders that more takeovers were underway and two were near completion. He hoped the company would obtain a full stock market share quote before the end of the year.

Sir Fred created the Pontin's holiday camp group which is now owned by the Bass brewing company. He left the company shortly after he sold out in 1978.

However, Sir Fred, an ebullient character retaining much of his holiday camp image, has no intention of getting involved in his old business in his career comeback, saying, 'They are too down-market these days'.

Kunick will concentrate on other leisure areas. Its present activities include discotheques, public houses and a theatre.

Don Robinson, who rescued Hull City football club from bankruptcy, is impressed by the potential of theme parks. Kunick is as present negotiating for a site to build a compact, undercover park in central London.

The Robinson family, Sir Fred, and Trident TV are the main Kunick shareholders. Sir Fred's share stake based on the 20p price the shares have commanded in unofficial dealings, is valued at about £600,000.'

*

From the Scarborough Evening News:

'In July 1983 Leisure company chiefs Sir Fred Pontin and Don Robinson got together in Scarborough this week 25 years ago.

The two had just set up the National Leisure Group, with the holiday-camps king as chairman and Mr Robinson as the managing director.

The new company's assets included Scarborough's Royal Opera House, the nearby Showboat pub and the Coronia pleasure boat, and it also held shares in the Scene One and Two discos in Aberdeen Walk.

Sir Fred, on his first visit to Scarborough, was shown round by Mr Robinson – and said afterwards that he had been very impressed.'

# CHAPTER 11

# 1985 – Live Aid

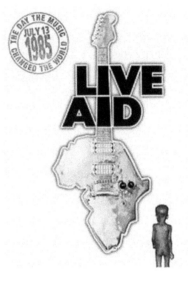

*Princess Diana who Don met,
and the Live Aid logo*

Whilst Don has been an extremely successful businessman in very varied spheres for over 55 years - he is the first to admit that without his businesses being successful he would not have been in a position to donate so generously to some very worthwhile causes. Live Aid was a case in point. Without success in many previous ventures Don would not have had the capital to enable Kunick to make a bid for Wembley Stadium.

Whilst it seems unlikely Kunick's bid was accepted, they did buy Allied Entertainments from Harvey Goldsmith's company and this company promoted the charitable Live Aid Concert for which 'a much reduced' rent for the use of Wembley Stadium for the UK part of the Live Aid concert was agreed. For the concert he was also appointed a Live Aid director.

As Don is the first to admit, such a prestigious position brings certain benefits. 'At the Live Aid Concert at Wembley Stadium I was honoured to meet Princess Diana, Elton John and many other well-known personalities. I was on the same row as Bob Geldorf and private boxes were also available.

*Top: Live Aid crowd; Bottom from the left: Jason Marshall (son of Don's friend Henry Marshall), Don's youngest son Andrew,*

*and Don.*

The 72,000 crowd was massive, the atmosphere

electric, and, knowing that up to 1.9 billion people would watch worldwide – the majority of course through TV; to me it felt as though Christmas had come early.'

Live Aid was a dual-venue concert held on 13 July 1985. The event was organised by Bob Geldof and Midge Ure to raise funds for relief of the ongoing Ethiopian famine. Billed as the 'global jukebox', the event was held simultaneously at Wembley Stadium in London, (attended by 72,000 people) and John F. Kennedy Stadium in Philadelphia, Pennsylvania, United States (attended by about 100,000 people). On the same day, concerts inspired by the initiative happened in other countries, such as Australia and Germany. It was one of the largest-scale satellite link-ups and television broadcasts of all time: an estimated global audience of 1.9 billion, across 150 nations, watched the live broadcast.

The 1985 Live Aid concert was conceived as a follow-on to the successful charity single 'Do They Know It's Christmas?' which was also the brainchild of Geldof and Ure. In October 1984, images of millions of people starving to death in Ethiopia were shown in the UK in Michael Buerk's BBC News reports on the 1984 famine. Bob Geldof saw the report, and called Midge Ure from Ultravox, and together they quickly co-wrote the song, 'Do They Know It's Christmas?' in the hope of raising money for famine relief. Geldof then contacted colleagues in the music industry and persuaded them to record the single under the title 'Band Aid' for free. On 25th November 1984, the song was recorded at Sarm West Studios in Notting Hill, London, and was released four days later. It stayed at number one for five weeks in the UK, was Christmas number one, and became the fastest-selling single ever in Britain and raised £8 million, rather than the £70,000 Geldof had expected. Geldof then set his sights on staging a huge concert to raise further funds.

The concert grew in scope, as more acts were added on both sides of the Atlantic. Hal Uplinger was the producer of the US part of the event. As a charity fundraiser, the concert far exceeded its goals: on a television programme in 2001, an organiser stated that while initially it had been hoped that Live Aid would raise £1 million with the help of Wembley tickets costing £25.00 each, the final figure was £150 million (approx. $283.6 million). Partly in recognition of the Live Aid effort, Geldof received an honorary knighthood from the Queen. Promoter Harvey Goldsmith also helped in bringing the plans of Geldof and Ure to fruition. For his contribution to Live Aid in the US, Uplinger won a 1989 Computerworld Smithsonian Award in the Media, Arts & Entertainment Category

The concert began at 12:00 BST (7:00 EDT) at Wembley Stadium in the United Kingdom. It continued at JFK Stadium in the United States, starting at 13:51 BST (8:51 EDT). The UK's Wembley performances ended at 22:00 BST (17:00 EDT). The JFK performances and whole concert in the US ended at 04:05 BST July 14 (23:05 EDT). Thus, the concert continued for just over 16 hours, but since many artists' performances were conducted simultaneously in Wembley and JFK, the total concert's length was much longer. It was the original intention for Mick Jagger and David Bowie to perform an intercontinental duet, with Bowie in London and Jagger in Philadelphia. Problems of synchronization meant that the only remotely practical solution was to have one artist, likely Bowie at Wembley, mime along to pre-recorded vocals broadcast as part of the live sound mix for Jagger's performance from Philadelphia. Veteran music engineer David Richards (Pink Floyd and Queen) was brought in to create footage and sound mixes that Jagger and Bowie could perform to in their respective venues. The BBC would then have had to ensure that those footage and sound mixes were in synch while also performing a live vision mix of the footage from both venues. The combined footage would then have had to be bounced back by satellite to the various broadcasters around the world. Due to the time lag (the signal would take several seconds to be broadcast twice across the Atlantic Ocean) Richards concluded there would be no practical way for Jagger to be able to hear or see Bowie's performance, meaning there could be no interaction between the artists, which would defeat the whole point of the exercise. On top of this both artists objected to the idea of miming at what was perceived as a historic event. Instead, Jagger and Bowie worked with Richards to create a video clip for the song they would have performed, a cover of 'Dancing in the Street'. The video was shown on the screens of both stadiums and also broadcast as part of many TV networks' coverage.

Each of the two main portions of the concert ended with their particular continental all-star anti-hunger anthems, with Band Aid's 'Do They Know It's Christmas?' closing the UK concert, and USA for Africa's 'We Are the World' closing the US concert (and thus the entire event itself).

Concert organizers have subsequently said that they were particularly keen to ensure that at least one surviving member of The Beatles, ideally Paul McCartney, took part in the concert as they felt that having an 'elder statesman' from British music would give it greater legitimacy in the eyes of the political leaders whose opinions the performers were trying to shape. McCartney agreed to perform and has said that it was 'the management' – his children – that persuaded him to take part. In the event, he was the last performer (aside from the Band Aid finale) to take to the stage and one of the few to be beset by technical difficulties; his microphone was turned off for the first two minutes of his piano performance of 'Let It Be', making it difficult for television viewers and impossible for those in the stadium to hear him. He later jokingly thought about changing the lyrics to 'There will be some feedback, let it be'.

Phil Collins performed at both Wembley Stadium and JFK, utilising Concorde to get him from London to Philadelphia. UK TV personality Noel Edmonds piloted the helicopter that took Collins to Heathrow Airport to catch his flight. Aside from his own set at both venues, he also provided drums for Eric Clapton and the reunion of the surviving members of Led Zeppelin at JFK. On the Concorde flight, Collins encountered actress and singer Cher, who later claimed not to know anything about the Live Aid concerts. Upon reaching the US however she did attend the Philadelphia concert and can be seen performing as part of that concert's "We Are the World" finale.

An official book was produced by Bob Geldof in collaboration with photographer Denis O'Regan.

## 'IT'S 12 NOON IN LONDON, 7 AM IN PHILADELPHIA, AND AROUND THE WORLD IT'S TIME FOR - LIVE AID ....' Richard Skinner opening the show.

The concert was the most ambitious international satellite television venture that had ever been attempted at the time. In Europe, the feed was supplied by the BBC, whose broadcast was opened by Richard Skinner, co-hosted by Andy Kershaw, and included numerous interviews and chats in between the various acts.

The Coldstream Guards band opened with the National Anthem, Status Quo started their set with 'Rockin' All Over the World', also playing 'Caroline' and fan favourite 'Don't Waste My Time'. This was to be the last appearance by the band to feature bassist and founder member Alan Lancaster, and drummer Pete Kircher who had joined the band three years earlier.

Queen galvanised the stadium with some of their greatest hits, in which lead singer Freddie Mercury at times led the entire crowd of 72,000 in thundering unison refrains. In their 20 minute set the band opened with 'Bohemian Rhapsody' and closed with 'We Are the Champions'. They extensively rehearsed their performance at London's Shaw Theatre. Prior to their taking the stage, Queen's sound engineer covertly switched out the limiters that had been installed on the venue's sound system so the performance would be louder than the others. Queen's performance on that day has since been voted by more than 60 artists, journalists and music industry executives as the greatest live performance in the history of rock music. Mercury and fellow band member Brian May later sang the first song of the three-part Wembley event finale, 'Is This The World We Created...?'

Bob Geldof himself performed with the rest of the Boomtown Rats, singing 'I Don't Like Mondays'.

Elvis Costello appeared singing a simple but touching version of The Beatles' 'All You Need Is Love', which he introduced by asking the audience to 'help [him] sing this old northern English folk song'.

U2's performance established them as a pre-eminent live group for the first time – something for which they would eventually become superstars. The band played a 14-minute rendition of 'Bad', during which lead vocalist Bono jumped off the stage to join the crowd and dance with a girl. The length of their performance of 'Bad' limited them to playing just two songs; the third, 'Pride (In the Name of Love)', had to be ditched. In July 2005, the girl with whom he danced revealed that he actually saved her life at the time. She was being crushed by the throngs of people pushing forwards; Bono saw this, and gestured frantically at the ushers to help her. They did not understand what he was saying, and so he jumped down to help her himself.

Another moment that garnered a huge crowd response was when David Bowie performed 'Heroes' and dedicated it to his son, as well as 'All our children, and the children of the world"

At the conclusion of the Wembley performances, Bob Geldof was raised heroically onto the shoulders of The Who's guitarist Pete Townshend and Paul McCartney – symbolising his great achievement in unifying the world for one day, in the spirit of music and charity.

Throughout the concerts, viewers were urged to donate money to the Live Aid cause. Three hundred phone lines were manned by the BBC, so that members of the public could make donations using their credit cards. The phone number and an address that viewers could send cheques to were repeated every twenty minutes.

Nearly seven hours into the concert in London, Bob Geldof enquired how much money had been raised; he was told £1.2 million.

The next day, news reports stated that between £40 and £50 million had been raised. Now, it is estimated that around £150m had been raised for famine relief as a direct result of the concerts.

# CHAPTER 12

## The Cricket Years

'The Centenary [Cricket] Festival in 1986 was the 100th staged at North Marine Road, Scarborough yet despite the celebrations for it, it was generally felt that the Festival was in decline. Membership, a reliable guide to cricket followers' optimism, had fallen dramatically by nearly one-third in the 1980s, from 3,067 in 1980 to 2,135 in 1985.

What was really needed was an injection of vitality and energy to set the wheels of expectation spinning again in the minds of Festival die-hards and casual watchers alike. Then, as always in the history of Scarborough Cricket Club, the right man appeared, at the right time. That man was Don Robinson.

Don Robinson had lived as a boy near the cricket ground. For many years he had been one of Scarborough's most prominent businessmen and entrepreneurs in the entertainment and tourist industry. The restoration of the Royal Opera House Theatre was one of his ventures, as was the establishing of the Zoo and Marineland, Mr Marvel's Funfair and Water Scene attractions on Scarborough's North Bay.

As chairman of Scarborough Football Club, he had been instrumental in putting that club on stable financial footing, from which base the club succeeded in reaching the FA Trophy Final at Wembley on three occasions in the 1970s, which nicely complemented the three successful visits to Lord's by Scarborough Cricket Club in the same decade.

The town certainly had outstanding publicity from its sporting successes in that era, although Robinson's attempt to interest the cricket club in a ground-sharing scheme at North Marine Road in 1979 was more a publicity venture than a practical reality. By the time Scarborough Football Club were promoted to the Football League in 1987, Robinson had moved on to become a director and chairman of Hull City Football Club, setting about the task on Humberside in the same vigorous manner that characterised his approach to his business affairs. An inspired committee decision meant that Robinson was invited to become president of Scarborough Cricket Club in 1988.

*

The invitation to Don Robinson was presented by Fred Robson, who had succeeded Geoffrey Smith as chairman of Scarborough Cricket Club in the previous year.

Smith, a former accountant, had been chairman of the club for seven years, having joined the committee in 1954 after being a playing member. He was another of the long-serving committee members so characteristic of the club's history and was also a member of the Yorkshire committee for several years. With his quiet, diplomatic and sometimes whimsical approach, he did much to continue the good relationship between the two clubs.

Fred Robson, too, is experienced in the ways of Scarborough Cricket Club. A Durham man and a useful club cricketer, he had played for Scarborough since 1963, joined the committee in 1968, was elected vice chairman in 1980, chairman in 1987 and had witnessed the changing face of Festival cricket and of Festival finances. More specifically, he recognised the necessity for the club to keep pace with modern developments in the entertainment and business worlds. It was from that perspective that Don Robinson was approached to become president of the club.

The list of past presidents of Scarborough Cricket Club is an imposing one. In modern times it features titled aristocracy like HRH The Duke of Edinburgh (1961), His Grace The Duke of Norfolk (1963), HRH The Duchess of Kent (1976), to set alongside cricket notables like Brian Sellers (1965), Herbert Sutcliffe (1968) and Sir Leonard Hutton (1975, 1986).

With due respect to those worthy individuals, it is unlikely that any of them had as much impact on the club as Don Robinson.

Robinson made it abundantly clear from the outset that he was going to be a 'hands-on' president and not simply a figurehead; and was as good as his word. By making use of a vast number of associates in the business and entertainment industries, he jolted any suspicion of complacency out of the Scarborough Cricket Club system and created a 'buzz' reminiscent of the arrival of `Alfie' Rutherford forty years before.

The Festival woke up with a start. A sense of expectation filled the air. An 'atmosphere' was rekindled. People were talking again with optimism. In modern marketing language, the realisation that the Festival was an entertainment product to be sold in a competitive outside world market, was brought forcefully to the attention of anyone remotely connected with the club.

Not that tradition was abandoned, or even overlooked. It was skilfully adapted to the present requirements, as Robinson resurrected one of the major social occasions of yesteryear, the Festival Banquet. Major civic and sporting dignitaries were invited to what proved to be a substantial fund-raising affair. Thanks to Robinson's organising abilities, a splendid dinner-dance was held in the Festival marquees to the accompaniment of a monster firework display on the ground, whilst as a real echo of times past, the London Stock Exchange played a match against a Yorkshire League XI as a curtain raiser to the 1988 Festival.

Not only that, but Robinson reinstituted the tradition led by CI Thornton, HDG Leveson-Gower, TN Pearce and latterly DB Close, of the invitation team for the three-day match carrying the name of a team organiser and so Michael Parkinson's World XI took the field against MCC in 1988 and 1989 and against India in 1990.

Don Robinson clearly had a major role to play in the areas of sponsorship, advertising and the media. He was quickly able to secure the agreement of Tesco Stores Ltd to sponsor a three-day international match at the Festival and for Ward's Buildings to take over the sponsorship of the four counties knock-out tournament, originally the Fenner Trophy, which had been continued by Asda Stores Ltd and was the centrepiece of the modern Festival, at least as far as gate receipts were concerned.

Other major sponsors like Joshua Tetley and McCain Foods (GB) Ltd were attracted, joining longer-established local sponsors like Plaxtons and the Scarborough Building Society in being associated with the Scarborough Cricket Festival. Boundary-board advertising suddenly became in greater demand as Yorkshire Television was persuaded to cover extensively not only the Festival but also Yorkshire matches at North Marine Road. The television company also sponsored the Festival Banquet and few days were allowed to pass without some items of news about the Festival appearing in different branches of the media.

Such items ranged from team news and ticket prices, to the state of the wicket and the installation of new seats in the North Stand for the greater comfort of spectators.

*Guests at the 1988 Festival Dinnner. From left to right: Don Robinson, (president of Scarborough CC); the late Gilbert Gray QC (speaker); Michael Parkinson; David Kendall (speaker); Lord Mountgarret (president of Yorkshire CCC); Councilor G. Allison (mayor of Scarborough)*

As in the days of Robert Baker, WW Leadbeater and `Alfie' Rutherford, Don Robinson had command of the details.

The Robinson effect was far more than the stiff breezes and bracing climate for which Scarborough is noted. It was a whole gale force which produced a stimulating and confidence-building response in committee, members and public alike. The only requirement for presidents in the past had been to make at least one appearance at the Festival, but Robinson's involvement was year-long and practical.

Expectations were heightened as the quality of teams to play at the Festival was announced and major sponsors obtained. From a surplus figure of £7,510 in 1987, profits rocketed to £28,270 in 1988.

Only twice since World War Two has the president of Scarborough Cricket Club been invited to serve a second successive term of office, but is unlikely that many voices were raised in objection when the committee invited Don Robinson to continue in 1989. The financial results were just as impressive as the previous year, with income up to £144,516 and profits at £28,068. In 1990, Robinson was elected a vice president of the club.

The 1980s had finished with a bang and another high profile figure became president in 1990. Michael Parkinson, invited by Robinson to front the invitation team at the Festival, presided over another financially successful year as profits of £30,914 accrued in a period of general recession.

When income from the Jack Knowles Deceased Trust is added, Scarborough Cricket Club was able to look forward to the 1990s with much greater optimism than had been the case even five years earlier. In 1991 the policy of an actively involved president was continued as Charles McCarthy, deputy chairman of McCain Foods (GB) Ltd, attended three-quarters of scheduled committee meetings, a commitment well beyond the call of duty for earlier presidents.

The present administration of Scarborough Cricket Club is well aware that it has much to do if the Festival and the club are to prosper in the twenty-first century. Scarborough Cricket Festival is an accepted part of cricket and has given great pleasure to a vast number of people.

Those people who have contributed over the years, in the words of Jim Kilburn *have painted a corner on the canvas of a nation's life, and added their mite to the sum of human happiness..'*

*

Don Robinson remembers, as a schoolboy, helping out at the Scarborough Cricket Club Ground. One of his jobs was to clean the dressing rooms and assist the cricketers with their kit and at one Festival (now the late Sir) Don Bradman was playing. Don says 'in my eyes he was like a God.'

Don was warned that Bradman had a firm policy - he never gave out autographs or signed autograph books and as most people at the ground knew this there was likely to be trouble if anyone upset Bradman by asking.

One day at end of play Bradman asked Don to take his cricket bag back to the Royal Hotel where he was staying. 'Ask for me at reception he said, and I might have a big surprise for you.'

Don did so and was felt he was in in heaven when Bradman rewarded Don with his autograph.

*

Celebrity cricket-lover Michael Parkinson bowled a bouncer at Scarborough Cricket Festival's organisers as the 105th festival started.

The chat-show host and writer launched a stinging attack on the organisers in an article in the Daily Telegraph.

Mr Parkinson had become involved in the festival three years before when businessman Don Robinson was President of the club for 2 years and Mr Parkinson followed him for a year. His name was attached to a World XI playing in the event.

Mr Parkinson said in his article that before Mr Robinson became involved the festival 'had all the allure of a turnip-growing contest'.

By 1991 Mr Robinson had retired as festival president, and Mr Parkinson, who had completed his term as president which followed Don's, said that 'the men who know about turnip-growing competitions are back in charge'.

The broadcaster also claimed that his name had been dropped from the title of the World XI at the last moment because the organisers wanted to create a team under the name of cricket-loving Prime Minister John Major.

Later, in an interview with the Scarborough Evening News, Mr Parkinson said: 'The same people that created the cock-up that Don Robinson sorted out are back in charge at Scarborough.'

*

## 2010 –The Scarborough Evening News reported:

'A former president of Scarborough Cricket Club has revealed he is bowled over by the redevelopment of the town's famous North Marine Road ground in 2010.

Don Robinson, who presided over the club's famous annual cricket festival, has tipped the renovation to herald a tourist boom in Scarborough.

The work, which was being carried out to coincide with the 125th anniversary of the festival, includes improvements to the pavilion and its windows, with the demolition and replacement of existing toilets on the east terrace and alterations to the ticket office. A new shop adjoining the new toilet block will also be installed.

Mr Robinson said: 'I'm so pleased and it is unbelievable to see the work happening. Scarborough Cricket Club is internationally famous. I went to a Sir Donald Bradman museum in Australia and Scarborough got a lot of mentions about the cricket club and the festival.

Everyone in Scarborough should be pleased too, it is good for the town, for the council, the shop-owners, hoteliers and the bar owners.

It is good for Scarborough as it will mean that people from all around the area and from across the UK will want to come here and watch the cricket.

Bill Mustoe, Tony Gibson, Colin Adamson and the whole organisation at the club is fantastic and I'm delighted this work is going on.'

Mr Robinson, who, during his time as president was only the third person to be asked to do it two years running, said he believed Scarborough was now fit to host one-day international matches, and was key to boosting the town's tourism profile.

However, he said the town was still in need of one added feature - a new bypass on the A64 to avert a bottleneck of traffic heading into town during busy periods.

He added: "Scarborough is on a real boom. We have the best resort in the UK which is showing the way forward.

We have the North Marine Drive, the Spa and the Open Air Theatre and I think that is going to bring a lot of people to the town.

We have got to bring forward the improvements on the road and the Government should be looking at it so the traffic misses the villages and there are no bottlenecks.

I hope Robert Goodwill will look at it and see if he can put it on the priority list because it would attract a lot more people to the town.

This year will see the ground host the 125th anniversary of the annual cricket festival, which has attracted some of the finest players in the sport's history.'

## DON VALLEY STADIUM – Floodlit Cricket 11th August 1992

The following comment online led me to undertake further research.

'I vaguely remembered a floodlit match [a cricket match] - it was over 20 years ago! So I looked it up - they played - under lights - for the Flamingoland Trophy.'

Research showed the match was between Yorkshire and Durham and Yorkshire won by 8 wickets. Don thought it was the first floodlit game of cricket in the UK although this is disputed in the press cutting below so it could have possibly been the first floodlit cricket match at Don Valley Stadium, Sheffield, which had been built in September 1990 for £29m. The stadium was demolished in September 2013. It had a capacity of 50,000 for concerts, 25,000 for other events, but 'only' 10,000 for football.

*

'Don Robinson stitched the floodlight cricket deal together. He had television contacts and persuaded ITV to cover the event live. To attract them further he offered not to make a transmission charge providing the programmers would televise adverts for the fixture for many weeks before it was due to take place.

This was all eventually agreed and thousands of tickets were sold in advance of the fixture.

Don estimates a crowd of around 15,500 was present and thought it was the first ever UK floodlit cricket match.'

*

However, research indicates that the first cricket match to be played under floodlights took place on 11 August 1952, at 7.30pm between Middlesex County Cricket Club and Arsenal Football Club. 'That match was a benefit for Jack Young. Lighting had been installed at Arsenal's Highbury ground in the summer of 1951, and this was first used for floodlit football in October 1951.

The cricket match took place a year later on 11th August 1952 at 19.30, the lights being turned towards the end of the first innings, in which Arsenal was batting.

A public announcement was made, advising spectators (of which there were just over 7,000) to 'Keep your eye on the ball. When you see it coming keep low. The batsmen will try to keep it down but they can't promise.' The match was televised on the BBC, with over a million viewers tuning in to watch the spectacle. *The Times* was not convinced of the success of floodlights in cricket, mischievously asking: 'What is to prevent non-stop Test matches where the last wicket falls as the milkman arrives?'

*

Don Valley stadium was once considered a symbol of a bright new Sheffield – 'it looks as though it has just landed,' a newspaper noted the week it opened in 1990 and it was the first national sports ground built in the UK since Wembley in the 1920s.

The 25,000 capacity facility became Britain's biggest athletics venue and would go on to inspire a future Olympic hero, while also hosting everything from football, rugby and cricket to concerts by global pop superstars such as Michael Jackson.

Now, the Attercliffe venue once considered to be the future, will be consigned to the past. Work began to demolish the £29 million stadium in 2013 as part of austerity cuts by Sheffield City Council.

'It's a world class facility,' says Rob Creasey, head coach there since 2000 and leader of the recent Save Don Valley Campaign. 'Getting rid of it makes no sense. This is a city asset. It has such a great history.'

Certainly there can be little doubt about that history.

Sheffield's 2012 Olympic hero Jessica Ennis-Hill first got into track and field after attending a sports day there; double Olympic gold-winner Dame Kelly Holmes ran her last race on the track; and Oliver Pistorius competed in one of his first major non-disabled runs at the facility.

Famously, Czech javelin thrower Jan Zelezny set a world record on the field – and almost speared a trackside TV interviewer while doing so.

Away from sport, it holds the record for Sheffield's biggest gig when 55,000 turned up to watch Michael Jackson in 1997. Def Leppard and The Rolling Stones have also headlined. 'People often think it's just an athletics stadium," says Rob. "But that's wrong. It's also the finest performance arts space in Yorkshire.'

The stadium was originally built as part of a £147 million transformation of Sheffield ahead of the World Student Games. Speaking ahead of its opening, MP Richard Caborn called it 'a jewel in the city's crown'.

Sheffield Eagles and Rotherham FC have both called it home while American football's BritBowl has been hosted there. In the UK's first ever floodlit cricket match Yorkshire took on a World XI in August 1991. It was once even mooted as a potential shared ground for Sheffield Wednesday and Sheffield United.

*Don Valley Stadium, Sheffield 1990*

It included the brightest floodlights ever installed in the UK and a track designed to help runners achieve personal best times.

It remained the biggest athletics venue in the country until London's Olympic Stadium was opened.

Improvements announced in 1994 would have made it even larger. In those proposals grandstands would have been built on all four sides.

The plans were shelved – temporarily, it was said – due to lack of finance.

Not that that stopped the big events coming. Athletics, Grand Prix, the Sheffield Half Marathon and several showpiece rugby games were all regularly held there. As late as summer 2013, it hosted the British Transplant Games and Scout-tastic, a jamboree attended by 6,000 scouts.

And yet, despite its history, Sheffield City Council announced in January the stadium was to be knocked down. Officials said it would save £700,000 annually, while declaring the smaller (and upgraded) Woodbourn Road athletics track would prove an adequate replacement. They pointed out spectator numbers, even for the biggest athletic meetings, were low.

Despite opposition – including a petition signed by almost 6,000 people – the stadium demolition went ahead.

'It was a sad day,' says Rob. 'Don Valley Stadium should be part of Sheffield's future.'

Whilst Don Robinson's flood lit cricket at Don Valley was held on the 11th August 1992, only two weeks later for two nights on 24th and 25th August he organised further Floodlit Cricket at Gateshead International Stadium.

On 24th August the match was between West Indies V the Rest of the World. We have not been able to trace the result.

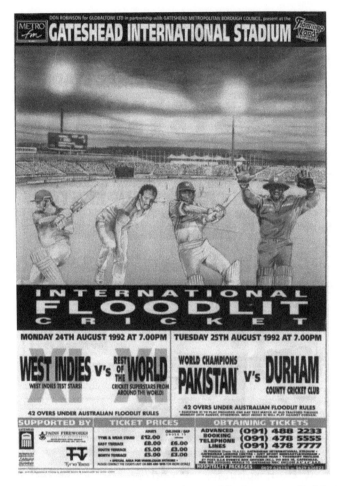

The result of the match on the 25th August, Pakistan – then World champions - against Durham led to Pakistan winning by 58 runs.

The Pakistanis then moved on to North Marine Road Scarborough for a 3 day match between 26th and 28th August against the World. This match was drawn.

# CHAPTER 13

## 1990s - THE HULL KINGSTON ROVERS YEARS

Hull Kingston Rovers or Hull KR ('The Robins') is a professional rugby league football club. The club formed in 1882 and currently competes in Super League, having won promotion from National League One in 2006. Hull KR is one of two professional rugby league teams in the city along with Hull FC.

When the league resumed in 1945 after World War II Rovers finished 18th out of 27. By 1959/60 the club had moved up to 13th out of 30. This was the first time the club had finished in the top half of the table since 1930/31 and the players shared a bonus of £500.

In 1961/62, the club won 17 successive matches and finished 8th out of 30.

Huddersfield and Hull Kingston Rovers met at Headingley, Leeds, in the first final of the Eastern Division Championship on Saturday 10th November. Reigning champions, Huddersfield were favourites to lift the Eastern Division title, especially as Rovers were missing five first choice players with injuries. The Robins, however, set the early pace and were 10–0 up after 30 minutes. Despite a rally by Huddersfield, Rovers hung on to win 13–10. This was Rovers first trophy for more than 30 years.

In the early 1970s Hull KR purchased a site at Winchester Avenue with the aim of building a new stadium. The plans never came to fruition and the site was later sold to a private developer. The profit made from this land was used to buy back Craven Park with greyhound racing continuing as a subsidiary concern.

The New Zealand team visited Craven Park on the 8th September 1971. The Kiwis, playing their third game in five days, were unable to match the Robins, who beat the Kiwis 12–10.

Moving forward, George Fairbairn was brought in as a player-coach in 1992 for a record fee of £72,500 but in 1994/5, the team was relegated to the third division despite finishing mid table.

Rovers were again crowned champions of the now renamed Second Division in 1996 and were this time promoted to the First Division. Rovers made some impact in 1997 and finished 8th. They also won the only Challenge Cup Plate beating Hunslet Hawks 60–14 at Wembley.

Rovers finished second in the league in 1998, and came close to a Grand Final spot with a Super League spot at stake. The Robins were expected to go one better in 1999 and topped the table for most of the season before their run ended and the final six games saw them drop from first place to sixth, missing out on a play-off place. Disappointment followed the year after when they finished in seventh place in the league after a mid-season collapse and exited the play-offs in the first round.

*

Don Robinson must have had rugby in his blood. His father, Joe had been a rugby league international and played for Batley, Bradford Northern and Rochdale Hornets.

Don played as a full back for Scarborough and interest had been shown by other clubs. In 1957 an approach was made by Hull KR who wanted to sign him professionally. They agreed an undisclosed three figure fee, bought him a house in Scarborough – until then he had been running a fish and chip shop and living above the premises, and agreed he could train at the  Scarborough ground. Don travelled to Hull for matches playing for KR between 1957 and 1960 but says 'he wasn't very good'.

In 2000 Robinson took over the Greyhound racing at Hull's Craven Park which had been a subsidiary activity of the club. He gave the Craven Park Stadium 'an expensive facelift' and the crowds flocked back to watch the twice weekly greyhound race nights from the improved facilities which included restaurants, bars, television screens and full Tote betting.

Only a year later in 2001 Robinson took control of Hull KR as Chairman, and Gary Wilkinson became head coach. Despite reaching the National Cup final and finishing fourth in the league, Wilkinson made way for the club's first overseas coach, Steve Linnane.

Under Linnane, the Robins came within eighty minutes of their first Grand Final appearance in 2002, after a largely successful end to the season, while the arrival of former player Nick Halafihi as chief executive, boosted the club's off-field activities.

Don resigned as chairman in June 2002.

In 2004 the club appointed Mal Reilly as Director of Rugby and Martin Hall as first team coach after Steve Linnane's resignation. But Reilly left the club mid-way through the season, while Hall took the club to the play-off semi-final before leaving once the season had finished. Halafihi also left the club.

Up to that time and unbeaten in their 2006 fixtures, in early June they were drawn to meet Super League side Warrington Wolves, in the quarter final of the Challenge Cup. It was arguably their biggest fixture for some years. Against all the odds the Robins won, 40–36, their best result in the competition since their 1980 Challenge Cup win against local rivals Hull F.C. This result also created a new club record of 18 consecutive wins. The victory set up a semi-final tie against Super League leaders, St Helens.

Rovers also progressed to the final of the Northern Rail Cup for the second successive season, against Leigh Centurions at Bloomfield Road, Blackpool on 16th July. Leigh Centurions won this game 22–18, thus ending Rovers' twenty four match unbeaten run. The club's Challenge Cup campaign also came to an abrupt halt, Rovers gamely succumbing 50–0 to triple-winning St Helens at The Galpharm Stadium, Huddersfield.

September 2006 saw Rovers crowned National League One Minor Premier winners, and qualify for an automatic place in the NL1 play-off semi-final at Craven Park against Widnes Vikings whom they beat 29–22 to reach the first Grand Final in their history, which they won 29–16, earning a place in the following season's Super League competition.

Hull KR made significant changes to their squad for the 2008 season, which saw eleven new players brought in and a number of players released or sold.

2009 saw further consolidation of Hull KR's Super League status with away victories at St Helens, Wigan and Warrington in a seven match winning run, taking Rovers briefly to the top position in the table.

2011 saw the end of Justin Morgan's reign as head coach and the club appoint Craig Sandercock as the new head coach for the 2012 season.

The team finished 10th in Sandercock's first season as a head coach and then made the playoffs in 2013, finishing 8th.

# CHAPTER 14

# 1990 - THE BULGARIAN YEARS

The following report appeared in Amusement
Business in May 1991:
'Don Robinson – Pilgrim Father

*Don Robinson is a man with a mission. Not satisfied with his success in Western Europe, he is now pioneering amusements further East.'*

'Don Robinson likes to compare the countries that used to comprise the Eastern Bloc, to the Wild West. Which makes him a pilgrim father. For Don Robinson is about to become the first British gaming and casino operator to set up in Bulgaria. Robinson has just won permission to develop Bulgaria's fourth casino allied to a 50 plus machine arcade in the heart of Bulgaria's capital Sofia. He has been working on the project for a year and has proved that post-Eastern bloc bureaucracy is surmountable. He is ahead of his field.

Robinson likes to remain low-profile, but is actually founder and deputy chairman of MHG and Bell-Fruit Services parent company Kunick plc.

Kunick is by no means the limit of his business activities. His life story presents a blueprint for the more entrepreneurial. Virtually everything he has ventured into thus far has turned to gold, which bodes well for the east. 'It is like Spain 25 years ago,' he says. 'It is exciting – especially for the machine business.'

His partner in the Bulgarian venture is Gary Scott, who has 16 arcades in Scotland.

*The Novotel, Sofia, Bulgaria (back left) where Don Robinson's company received a license to operate a casino in the Novotel hotel.*

Thus far, neither BFS nor MHG is involved in Robinson's project, but that does not rule out a role for either in the future. 'Naturally it is something that would be offered first to Kunick', he says.

Robinson's family holding company has set up in Bulgaria to develop and operate the casino, to be housed in the largest hotel in the city, the Novotel. Last year, [1990] 120,000 people visited the Novotel and 100,000 of these were westerners. Half of the total were Greeks, renowned for their enjoyment of gambling. The casino will, in keeping with the feel of the hotel, be based on a Las Vegas design – it will indeed be named after that gambling Mecca – 'which we think will have a lot of pull', says Robinson. It will contain a separate arcade with upwards of 50 machines. There is no legislation allowing for stand-alone arcades yet, but in a country where legislation is moving to capitalism closer by the day, this may not be far away.

Robinson watched legislation change to work in his favour as he negotiated with the Bulgarian authorities. Negotiation was, at times, tortuous but ground-breaking and definitely worth it now that he has become the first Brit to be allowed to operate a tourist company there. 'It takes a long time,' he says. 'It is a matter of gaining their confidence. There is legislation but that can change very quickly. A lot of their tax laws are very similar and there is a lot more bureaucracy, though and no one really wants to make a decision.' He continues, 'But when they realise that you want to do things and do things right, they are very helpful and start to suggest ways around things. Bulgaria is a very nice country with very nice people. In five years' time it will be a boom country for tourism – like Spain and Portugal are now.'

Robinson found that negotiation had to be both flexible and creative. The Bulgarian authorities wanted a British football club to visit so he arranged and paid for Hull City to go over – he was once chairman of the club. The authorities naturally wanted some television tourism coverage so Robinson, who has connections, immediately sold the idea on to Yorkshire Television. 'Other people who go out will have to realise there will be a lot of frustration, a lot of the time', he warns. 'They've got to win trust first.'

But Robinson has already done that and is ahead of the field to scoop the rewards as the barriers fall. Many have already been removed. Early anxieties about currency seem to have largely disappeared as the authorities have realised it is in their interest to compete with the black market and have legislated accordingly. Tokens are already established as gaming machine currency. The big boost will come when native Bulgarians are themselves allowed to gamble and legislation allowing this is near. Robinson doesn't see shortages, particularly of cash, as a problem. 'There are shortages out there. The people realise that and accept it, but money is still about. Even so, when cash is short there are people about. It reminds me of Britain after the war. There are a lot of budding entrepreneurs out there. Particularly in Sofia.' At the moment though not many of these are British and Robinson feels that we may be missing out. 'I think there would be potential for British manufacturers. It is surprising: the Spanish and Germans are there in a reasonable way, but have we got the get up and go in this country? Since I've opened up in Paris, I've come to realise just how far we are behind the continentals.' He says 'we' out of politeness but what he really means is 'you'. I can't imagine Don Robinson being second in any race.'

## ON 6TH JUNE 1996 THE SCARBOROUGH EVENING NEWS REPORTED: Raven Hall Hotel Gets Fit For Euro 96

'The owner of the Raven Hall hotel in Ravenscar, North Yorkshire, has pushed the boat out for her latest guests - a 40-strong delegation of footballers from Bulgaria.

The entourage, which arrives today to take part in the Euro96 football championships, has a new gym to work out in and a mini football pitch.

Doreen Gridley, owner and managing director of Raven Hall, admitted: 'I don't know one side of a football pitch from the other.' But that hasn't stopped her investing thousands of pounds for the team.

Ms Gridley brought forward the building of the gym specifically for the footballers. It was finished this week at an estimated cost of £8,000 - £10,000.

Scarborough Borough Council is understood to have put up £3,000 - £4,000 to meet the cost of the temporary football pitch, which is situated in an overflow car park.

The team, plus Football Association representatives, are taking over the 53-bedroom country house hotel for 13 nights, bringing it about £50,000 of business.

But the hotel has been spared the headache of coming up with a Bulgarian-themed menu - the team has brought its own Bulgarian chef, who will work with kitchen staff.

A number of other hoteliers in Scarborough have been left with empty rooms after hundreds of Bulgarian football fans cancelled their Euro96 visit because of a collapse in their currency.

David James, director of tourism and amenities at Scarborough Borough Council, said there would be 'a great deal less' turning up, but was unable to give exact figures.

Hoteliers this week remained philosophical, however. Frank White, owner of the Palm Court Hotel, who has lost more than £12,000 of trade after setting aside 17 of his 47 rooms, said: 'I would be more disappointed if I had given over all my rooms."

## THE CATERER AND HOTEL KEEPER REPORTED ON 11TH JUNE 1996:
## Scarborough content with Bulgarian support

An attempt by Scarborough Borough Council to bring foreign football followers to the seaside town and boost its economy has been branded a flop by Euro 96 officials, reports The Yorkshire Post.

The council is paying the £20,000 hotel bill for the Bulgarian team and £5,000 for training facilities, but the policy has only netted around 500 followers, compared with a hoped-for 5,000, says the paper.

A devaluation of the Bulgarian currency has not helped, but most Bulgarians are staying nearer where the actual matches are being played.

A spokesman for the Football Association said: 'It does seem to have been something of a flop for Scarborough. We would have preferred the team to stay elsewhere from the outset for obvious logistical reasons. It is a long, long way from the grounds at Newcastle and Elland Road [Leeds].

But Scarborough Council leader Mavis Don said: 'As far as I am concerned everything over 400 is a bonus since 400 was the worst case scenario.'

Scarborough tourism director David James said in February that 400 supporters would be worth £600,000 to the economy.'

Over the years Don Robinson has had many business interests in Bulgaria which include opening the Las Vegas Casino. He is extremely positive about the country and its people and he was awarded the Businessman of the Year Award in the late 1990s, by the Bulgarian TV & Radio network.'

\*

Before the football visit, The Mayor of Sofia, Stefan Sofianski extended the warm hand of friendship to the people of Scarborough.

In a message to his Scarborough counterpart, Councillor Ian Stubbs, Mr Sofianski said he hoped the visit would help to forge close links between the two countries.

'I would like to send my greetings to England and especially to my colleague Councillor Stubbs, in Scarborough', he said.

'I want to thank him for what he has done for the visit of the fans of the Bulgarian football team.

I hope this will help the good relationships, not just between Bulgaria and England, but between Sofia and Scarborough.

And I hope that the hospitality of the people of Scarborough will help to power us to victory.'

\*

Viktor Sergiev is a Bulgarian who came to England to study after the Eastern bloc regime fell in Bulgaria. He acted as an interpreter between the Bulgarians and the British when the Bulgarian Football team visited Scarborough prior to Euro 1996. Viktor writes:

'In 1993, four years after the Eastern bloc regime in Bulgaria joined the west I was accepted at Wyke College in Hull to do my A levels. The UK was the first country I ever went to and with only £600, which was all my parents' savings, I decided at the age of 16 to take the risk of living on my own in the search of a better life. There was a political turmoil, severe financial crises; food and fuel shortages in Bulgaria at the time and my parents were struggling financially. I managed to find the Jacob's Well Appeal charity in Beverley and Wyke Sixth Form College which were willing to support me, to cover my college fees and to provide accommodation and food. It was not an exciting college life being on my own and aiming to be the best student was the only chance I had to make it to a good University. In 1995 I graduated with straight "A" grades and I had to work for a year and write to hundreds of companies in order to be able to find financing for my University degree.

It was during that year 1996 when the Bulgarian Football team participated in the European Championship that I met Don Robinson. I volunteered as an interpreter and I met an exceptional UK individual who discovered Bulgaria and wanted to raise its profile in the UK by helping our national football heroes.

On many occasions after that year, I have approached Don for advice and help and on many occasions his goodwill and positive energy has given me hope that I could make it one day, despite the sacrifice of many years of an isolated hard life in the first few years in the UK.

Don Robinson is one of the very few people that has since that day been an exceptional ambassador of Bulgaria and has helped many Bulgarians. His business and charity initiatives should not to be forgotten. On a few occasions he has made the necessary referrals to help me deal in difficult situations and I could only say that I am very lucky to have known him over the years.

I have managed to persevere and graduate in BA Economics at Cambridge University where Churchill College provided me with a financial grant, allowing me to finish successfully my studies. I was one of the very few at the time who managed to get a job at UBS in London where I started my career as a banking analyst and subsequently as a proprietary trader.

I have taken managerial positions at HSBC London and Dresdner Bank in London.

I have established like Don many bridges between Bulgaria and the UK and I have managed to successfully bring large businesses to Bulgaria that have created hundreds of jobs in what I believe is a country with great potential now part of the EU.'

A Bulgarian newspaper giving details of their team and the Raven Hall at Ravenscar, Scarborough, where they stayed, with Don, centre right.

## Football Footnote:

In 1996, the Bulgarian football team qualified for the European Football Championship for the first time, after some good results in the qualifying group, including a stunning 3–2 turnaround win against future Euro 1996 champions Germany.

They were drawn in Group B with France, Spain, and Romania. Bulgaria started with a 1–1 draw against Spain, followed by a 1–0 win against Romania.

In the final group match, they lost 3–1 against France. At the same time, Spain defeated Romania 2–1 with the winner coming in the 84th minute, and the Bulgarians subsequently failed to qualify to the quarter-finals.

## John Woodcock, Yorkshire Post Magazine October 2nd 2004 wrote:

'In 2004 in Don Robinson's modest office in Westborough, Scarborough he passes over a letter from the Bulgarian Ambassador in London. There is another from a retired British Army general who can arrange for a member of the Royal Family to officially open Robinson's latest business venture in the Balkans.

It's a health spa in the mountains and will complement the casino his family operated in Sofia, where he is negotiating to run all the car parks in Bulgaria's capital for an outlay of £10m.

Robinson was the first entrepreneur in the previous Eastern bloc state. This is no great surprise when you study his track record. Innovation and gambling with ideas, have been an instinct for nearly 50 years – he pioneered commercial zoos and floodlit cricket in this country, and package tours to Las Vegas that cost 94 guineas.'

\*

In 1998 Don was appointed 'Businessman of the Year' in Bulgaria by the country's National Radio and TV network.

He was also nominated, and subsequently elected as a director of the British Bulgarian Chamber of Commerce for which the following statement was provided:

The Robinson Group of Companies is a holding company which combines my various companies and activities in the UK. The Robinson Group has been present in the Bulgarian market since 1990.

As then Chairman [of Hull City FC] I originally brought over Hull City to Bulgaria at my own expense after a Bulgarian team had not been able to pay the costs for another English Club to visit. The trip was the feature of a Yorkshire Television documentary.

At the time I was deputy Chairman of Kunick PLC, one of the UK's leading leisure and gaming firms which operated 40,000 slot machines in the UK and France. I received an offer for casino and slot machine operations at the Novotel, Sofia, Bulgaria during this period and entered in partnership with the Hotel, along with Kunick, who supplied many of the slot machines.

The Casino was opened in 1991 and we had many successful and happy years there. We employed on average 120 Bulgarians and paid approximately US$12m to the state in taxes and profit share from only 250 square metres of space. We were one of the leading corporate tax-payers in Bulgaria.

The casino ceased to operate after a privatisation deal in 1998.

In the past we have brought over UK investors from different sectors to introduce them to projects in Bulgaria and also helped with other projects in Bulgaria such as tourist-related projects in the Black Sea area and also in a small way, in the agriculture sector. We have also brought over six world-recognized surgeons from the UK and are currently organizing an exchange of nurses between the UK and Bulgaria.

We are currently actively working on some exciting projects in Bulgaria with well-known British partners in their field.

I am a Freeman of the City of Las Vegas, USA, a Freeman of the City of London, and also of my adopted home town Scarborough.

I was the Chairman of Hull Kingston Rovers Rugby Club, a Greyhound Racing Stud and am also vice-president of the London Stock Exchange Cricket Club which I have taken on tours of South Africa, Australia, Portugal and Gibraltar.

I have been a Barker of the Royal Variety Club of Great Britain for 35 years, which is the largest children's charity in the world.

I am very pleased to be asked to join the Board of the British Bulgarian Chamber of Commerce. We have always looked at Bulgaria over the longer term and would be very pleased to see it move forward in a positive manner. I would be very happy if I was able to help in some way after having experience in both countries, through involvement in investment projects and by attracting other UK investors to the country. Hopefully this would build mutual cooperation and respect on both sides.'

## The following release came from the Friends of Bulgaria:

'Don Robinson, a prominent British businessman and a true friend of Bulgaria has recently donated £10,000 for the work of Friends of Bulgaria.

He was also Chairman of the National Zoological Association of Great Britain between 1971-1982.

Don Robinson is a former President of the world-famous Scarborough Cricket Festival, and was co-founder and Deputy Chairman of Kunick Leisure Group Plc which, between 1982 - 1992, operated the leading Theme Parks and Zoos - Windsor Safari Park; Flamingo Land; and Dudley Zoo, Castle & Amusement Park. He is a former Director/Trustee of the Yorkshire Television Telethon Trust; has been a Barker of the Variety Club of Great Britain for over 30 years and for this he received The Variety Gold Heart Award in 1990. In 1985 Don was made a Freeman of the City of London.

He is also Vice President of the London Stock Exchange Cricket Club.

*Above: Don Robinson (right) pictured with the British Ambassador Roger Short MVO (left) who was later tragically killed in an attack on the British Embassy in Istanbul.*

Don has been actively involved in business projects in Bulgaria for several years as Chairman and Controlling Shareholder in Las Vegas Casinos Hotel Group in Bulgaria. He is Chairman of Sofiapark Group. During his career Don Robinson has also sponsored many charitable projects in Bulgaria. These include the provision of wheelchairs, hospital beds and medical equipment. Over the years he has been a strong supporter of Friends of Bulgaria.

Thank you, Don!'

*Bulgarian Teenager Ianitsa Paramove (centre) pictured with businessman Don Robinson (left) and Mike Kelly (right) at the CDS Transport depot where goods donated by Don's companies are about to be loaded for transporting to Bulgaria.*

*Don Robinson in front of the Las Vegas Hotel and Casino*

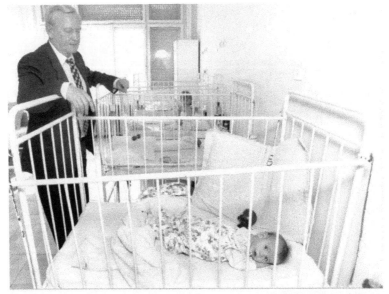

*Above: Don Robinson in the children's ward of the National Centre for Cardio-Vascular Diseases in Sofia. The children have all undergone cardio-vascular surgery.*

## From The Press, York 5<sup>th</sup> July 2006:
## 'Ambassador's visit boosts City's links to Bulgaria

'About 30,000 Britons have bought property in Bulgaria after visiting its capital, Sofia, and the Black Sea resorts. Around 6,000 of the buyers are from Yorkshire, more than any other part of the UK, according to businessman Don Robinson.

'Bulgaria is the hot new destination for holidaymakers and people seeking a bolthole, and the people who live there think Yorkshire is the capital of Britain.

That's why he and York inward investment chiefs organised a visit to the city for the eastern European country's top representative in this country.

Lachezar Matev, the Bulgarian ambassador to Britain, came to York with his wife and daughter, as part of a wider visit to the region.

*Lachezar Matev, the Bulgarian Ambassador to Britain, meets York's Lord Mayor, Janet Hopton.*

His party had a trip on the city's big wheel, during a visit to build better relations with the county.

The event was organised by Mr Robinson, a North Yorkshire businessman, in conjunction with the inward investment group www.york-england.com, to help foster relationships between Yorkshire and Bulgaria.

Mr Robinson said: 'The aim of this is to engender general relations across Yorkshire.

In Bulgaria, they think that the Yorkshire area is the capital of Britain. They played in the European Championships here in 1996 at Leeds United's ground, and they stayed in Scarborough, and we have had a lot of dignitaries and politicians visiting. People always love to come to York, and Yorkshire should be proud.'

Mr Matev and his family had afternoon tea in a civic reception with York's Lord Mayor, Janet Hopton, and her consort, before taking a spin on the Norwich Union Yorkshire Wheel.

The ambassador said: "I am enjoying the visit extremely well. I am very glad to be in the Yorkshire region for the first time.

'It's very important for us at this time of our preparation to join the European Union, to widen and develop regional contacts, and it's my personal challenge to be able to establish more contacts with the major and most important historic and economic cities in the UK."

Mr Matev's daughter, Emily, 17, who was given a brief tour of York, said: 'The atmosphere is just wonderful and it's a lovely place.'

Peter Wilkinson, vice-chairman of www.york-england.com, said: 'We are delighted that the ambassador has joined us. It's great for York and North Yorkshire.

'The investment opportunities for both Britain and Bulgaria are wonderful.

Don says, 'Bulgaria is a wonderful country and its people are so friendly and hard-working that we have been delighted to expand our businesses there. Both my sons live in Bulgaria to look after our business interests and I make frequent visits.'

*

Michael Day, now living in retirement in Helensburgh, Scotland has the final word in this chapter about Don's Bulgarian enterprises.

Michael had been in senior Management in some of the largest hotels in the UK when he got a call from Don Robinson asking whether he could give advice on hotel matters abroad.

The couple met and Don offered Michael a consultancy role in Don's hotel ventures in Bulgaria. Mike accepted and visited Bulgaria 3 or 4 times.

The first smaller casino was built as part of the existing Novotel Hotel. Then the new Las Vegas Casino and apartment block was built. Michael shares Don's enthusiasm for the country and its people and says,

'There is a saying that, if you find a good friend they are a friend for life.'

That is certainly true in Don's case. He approached me, I worked for him in a consultancy role, he helped me in my career, and he became a lifetime friend'.

*Lachezar Matev, the Bulgarian ambassador to Britain, held a Dinner at the Bulgarian Embassy in London. Don Robinson, his wife Jean, son Andrew and Andrew's wife Angelina were invited. Mr Matev appears 3rd left, Jean Robinson 1st left, Don Robinson 1st right and Andrew Robinson 3rd right. Unfortunately this photo shows only Angelina's hands, front right, so we include a photo of her below.*

Don sums up: 'In the 20 or so years I have been involved and of all the countries I have visited I am most impressed by the progress made by Bulgaria and its family-orientated people since they left the Eastern bloc. They study hard and are hardworking, pleasant and progressive people in their working lives. There are new hotels, apartment blocks, motorways and shopping malls and it is now an excellent country to visit, to live in or to expand a business into. Bulgaria is racing ahead and we have two or three new projects we are planning.'

# CHAPTER 15

# 1990 Winston Churchill's Britain at War, and
# The Dungeon years

## WINSTON CHURCHILL'S BRITAIN AT WAR

Another brainchild of Don Robinson's was his Winston Churchill's BRITAIN AT WAR Museum. This was a fantastic place which explained to young and old alike just what the war and Blitz were like to those living in cities. It was not just the bombing and the risk of death or injury to individuals, their families and friends, but the by-products of war – scarcity, rationing, women having to do men's work as the men were at war...

The following extract is taken from the Winston Churchill

Britain at War guide. Unfortunately this extremely popular event closed in 2014 as the property was leased from London Transport who wanted the site back for expansion of the adjoining underground station.

"The sinister wail of the air raid warning siren is the abiding memory of all who lived through the war. It indicated incoming bombers, often with only a few minutes warning. All those who could do so made for the nearest air raid shelter, and in London this was very often an underground station.

The first bombs fell on central London on August 24/25th, 1940, but what became known as the 'Blitz' started on September 7th, when the Battle of Britain was at its height. Some 375 Luftwaffe aircraft dropped bombs that evening, from Woolwich in the east to Westminster and Kensington in the west. The casualties totalled 306 dead and 1,337 injured. On the next two nights there were raids on an even greater scale with similar numbers of casualties. Night after night through September 1940 this mighty air assault on London continued, striking every kind of building indiscriminately with about 10,000 high explosive bombs and countless numbers of incendiary bombs. The Blitz continued with attacks on 57 consecutive nights until November 2nd, 1940, and then still regularly but with less terrifying intensity and frequency until May 10th, 1941. After this, occasional but still serious raids were made for the remainder of the war. In the first three months of the bombing 12,696 civilians were killed in the London region and around 20,000 were seriously injured.

In the face of all this it was Londoners themselves who took to seeking refuge in the Tube, simply by buying the cheapest ticket and settling down for the night with blankets, sleeping bags, and sandwiches on the platforms. In those stressful early days of September 1940 it was the logical thing to do.

Fortunately the authorities quickly accepted the idea as official policy. It had not been planned but soon they set up bunks, canteens, and toilet facilities to make the best of conditions. During September, too, the Aldwych branch of the

Underground below Kingsway was closed down and converted into one huge shelter with room for 8,000 people. So, in the winter of 1940-41, sleeping Underground became a way of life for thousands of Londoners.

No part of London was immune from bombing during the Blitz. Some 50,000 high explosive bombs were dropped between September 7th, 1940, and the end of July 1941.

Hundreds of thousands of incendiary bombs fell over the same period. These were non-explosive but burned fiercely and were intended to lodge in roof tops and start fires. The areas most seriously damaged by bombs included Poplar,Stepney, Bermondsey, Southwark, Deptford, Lambeth, Shoreditch, Bethnal Green, Holborn, the City, and the West End along the river through Westminster to Fulham. Major landmarks damaged included Buckingham Palace, the House of Commons, Somerset House, the Royal Courts of Justice, and the Guildhall. But St. Paul's Cathedral remained immune from damage throughout the Blitz and came to stand as a proud symbol of defiance and survival.

*St Paul's Cathedral during the Blitz*

Through the early weeks of the Blitz an average of 200 Luftwaffe aircraft bombed London each night, though totals engaged ranged from as few as 50 to as many as 400 on the night of October 15th, 1940, when 430 Londoners were killed and about 900 wounded. Faced with these attacks night after night, the air raid shelters became a way of life for those who stayed in London. As well as the Underground shelters there were 'communal' shelters for streets or areas, each holding 50 or more people.

These had been built for short term occupancy so they, too, had to have bunks and toilet facilities added for the all-night raids. But not everyone went to the shelters. Of 3,200,000 people in London in November 1940 only 300,000 took 'official' shelter of any kind. It was estimated that 1,150,000 took cover in 'private' shelters of the Anderson or basement type. Thus, of every 100 people in London, nine were in public shelters, 27 in 'private' shelters, and 64 not in shelters at all. Some of these 64 were civil defence personnel on duty, but others merely stayed in bed and took their chance or took refuge under the stairs at home. Public shelters were overcrowded in the early days but it was later estimated that there was public shelter space available for up to twice as many as actually used it.

Whether you stayed at home or went to a shelter, you could never predict what the morrow would bring. Somehow London carried on through the turmoil and everybody usually got to work against all odds, even if the workplace was destroyed during the night!

On a sombre note, the reassuring Underground shelters were not entirely immune from danger. They seemed safe because of their depth, but Marble Arch, Bank, and Balham stations were among those suffering under direct hits. At the Bank station 111 people were killed in January 1941.

The Defence Committee produced a report which greatly over-estimated the threat of German air power and predicted 60 days of intensive raids on London the moment war was declared, leading to a probable 450,000 deaths and one million injured.

Evacuation was, therefore, given a high priority in civil defence planning, and government departments and local government carved out extensive work during 1939 to identify 'safe' areas and establish the routes to be taken. Even billeting numbers were worked out for the various destinations, and a few special camps for evacuees were also built. Hence, when Germany invaded Poland on September 1st, 1939, and British involvement in the war became almost inevitable, the evacuation plan could be put into action that same day. Thousands of young children were escorted by their teachers and left the big cities for the countryside, mainly by train but also by bus and river steamer. They had with them a minimal change of clothes and necessities in a bag or case, their gasmask in its cardboard box, and an attached label giving their name, address, and destination. The whole operation took three days and the totals moved out from big cities all over Great Britain were 827,000 school age children, 103,000 teachers and social workers, 524,000 mothers and babies, 7,000 disabled people, and 13,000 expectant mothers. Some 48% of the school children of London were in this total.

This massive move was a triumph of organisation, but it led to considerable social upheaval and suffering for some, as poor children from inner city areas found themselves in unaccustomed surroundings and alien circumstances. More to the point the expected air assault did not take place, so there was some drift back to the cities as evacuation was not compulsory.

But this was reversed again when the bombing started in earnest in September 1940. Thereafter the number of evacuees rose and fell depending on the intensity of bombing at various times, but the biggest exodus of all took place in the summer of 1944 when the VI 'Buzz Bomb' attacks started on London and the South-East, followed in September by the devastating V2 assault. Over one and a half million people left the London area at this time, either officially or 'privately'.

'Private' evacuation, by those who had the means to

move out of London, was a particular feature of 1939-40 and 1944. Many houses in London were empty while hotels in the country did good business and there was a premium trade in country cottages. Some - including children - went to America or Canada for the duration of the war. To this must be added the evacuation of several government departments. Most of the BBC moved to Bristol, Evesham, and Bedford, and major London museums and art galleries whose treasures were taken off for safe storage. The National Gallery moved its priceless exhibits to a quarry in North Wales.

The major Blitz on London stretched from September 1940 to May 1941 with almost continuous nightly attacks. After this there were long periods of lull, but never a moment when vigilance could he relaxed. A major resurgence of activity came with the serious VI and V2 Blitz of 1944. London did not suffer alone. Almost every major city and industrial area in Britain was bombed at various times. The biggest provincial raid of all was the attack on Coventry on the night of November 14, 1940, when the centre of Coventry was almost completely destroyed by a force of about 400 aircraft, with heavy loss of life. Birmingham, Bristol, Liverpool, and Southampton all suffered major raids late in 1940.

Then Sheffield, Manchester, the naval ports, Clydeside, and Belfast were all hit heavily So it went on intermittently throughout the war, though the Luftwaffe's bombing strength was greatly dissipated after Germany's attack on Russia began in June 1941. In the later parts of the war small 'hit and run' sorties and 'nuisance raids' became the most common form of German attack.

Why Britain survived as well as it did was due to the excellent planning, organisation, training, and calibre of the civil defence forces. Britain was well prepared. The 'Air Raid Precautions' (ARP) system was started in September 1935 when it was realised that air power would be used in future conflicts on a hitherto unprecedented scale.

The Air Raid Wardens organisation started in April 1937 and planning for anti-gas measures, evacuation, ambulance and fire services, and air raid shelters all went swiftly ahead, spurred on by the use of air power seen in the Spanish Civil War and by the Munich Crisis of 1938. So, when war came, a complete ARP Service was already in being. The fire brigades were 'nationalised' as the National Fire Service (NFS) with a war service back-up called the Auxiliary Fire Service (AFS). A Police War Reserve and the Women's Voluntary Service, sponsored by the government was also formed. Information on the steps to take to cope with air attack, gas attack, blast or bomb damage was widely promulgated, all to be undertaken in strict blackout conditions!...'

## LONDON, YORK AND PARIS DUNGEONS

Don Robinson did not start the London Dungeon but he did develop it and set up other Dungeon experiences within the UK and Europe. The following extract from the Dungeons' guide highlights just a tiny part of what the dungeons are about and how barbaric a country we were in the past.

'Deep in the heart of London, buried beneath the paving stones of historic Southwark, lies the world's most chillingly famous museum of horror.

The London Dungeon brings more than 2,000 years of gruesome authentic history vividly back to life....and death.

As you delve into the darkest chapters of our grim and bloody past, recreated in all its dreadful detail, remember: everything you experience really happened.

The Middle Ages were a time of great upheaval throughout Europe, dominated by long periods of war and destruction...

...Despite a general belief that the 18th century heralded a new enlightened era in Europe, the hardship, poverty and authoritarian rule endured by the general populace differed little from that of earlier times.

Draconian justice was still the norm and the death sentence was available to judges for hundreds of different crimes, from sheep steeling to shop lifting.

In London the courts had never been busier. Typically the Old Bailey would be in session from early in the morning till late in the evening, hearing up to 20 cases a day.

Hangings would take place in busy town market places and in city centres. In London, Tyburn (close to where Marble Arch now stands) was the principal place of public execution; its triangular gallows could accommodate up to 21 people at once.

Those condemned were taken from Newgate and other prisons in open carts, followed by baying crowds.

For convicted traitors the punishment was even more horrific; hanging, drawing and quartering. The victim was first hanged, then disemboweled while still alive, and beheaded. Finally the body was hacked into four pieces and the parts taken back to the prison to be boiled before being put on public display.

Another traditional place for public executions was Tower Hill, just outside the walls of the Tower of London. Huge crowds would gather here and temporary stands had to be built to cope with the mass of spectators.

Only royal, aristocratic or important political figures were entitled to the dubious honour of travelling by barge through the infamous Traitors Gate to face the executioner within the precincts of the Tower itself, in relative privacy and away from public ridicule and humiliation...

...In the 1880's, the East End of London was a rather unpleasant place to live. High unemployment and low wages brought poverty and homelessness, and a general feeling of desperation pervaded the air.

As a result, people lived their squalid lives against a background of immorality, drunkenness, crime and violence. Robbery and assault were commonplace and the streets were ruled by gangs.

Then, between August 31st and November 9th 1888, there occurred a series of murders so gruesome, so evil that they outraged the entire nation. The killer was never found, but from those days forward, he was known as 'Jack the Ripper'.

Who was he? Where did he come from? Those are the questions detectives, criminologists and historians have been asking for over a century.

The slaughter of five prostitutes in the space of 10 weeks, all within a mile of each other spread fear and anger throughout Whitechapel. Police and vigilantes filled the streets and angry mobs attacked 'likely suspects'. The murderer was never found, despite the investigations of Inspector Abberline and his detectives from the Metropolitan Police. So who could have been Jack the Ripper?

Over the years there has been much speculation about his identity.

Whatever the truth, we shall probably never know, but more than a century later researchers are still uncovering more 'evidence' and trying to identify with certainty the mysterious killer of Whitechapel.

## From Leisure Week 7th September 1990
## Don Robinson answers questions:

'LW: *How do you decide whether a new idea is worth turning into a company?*

DR: I wouldn't like to do anything I couldn't make a profit

on; I'm profit oriented. I've had to be like that, because I've started my businesses up from scratch, so I've learnt the hard way. I've got it ingrained into me that we're there to make a profit. I am cost conscious, and go through figures with a fine toothcomb.

LW: *What is the key to the popularity of Kunick's London Dungeons?*

DR: You've got to make people feel part of the adventure. When you go round Disney and into Universal Film Studios, you feel part of the adventure, you're taking part in it and that's what we try to do at the Dungeons.

LW: *So, practically, how do you achieve this?*

DR: By good psychology, that is our business. It's trying to know what people want, and I feel we've got the right ingredients with our new exhibition, 'The Theatre of the Guillotine'.

Psychology is all about cultures, and entertainment is about psychology.

A lot of people think that leisure is easy, but leisure is a very, very hard business. You can lose a lot of money in it. People look and they think the money coming in through the doors is all big profit.

There's some big profits in leisure if it is run properly, but you've got to watch your overheads, the staffing levels and the advertising.

LW: *What are the prime difficulties in making a concept like the Dungeons profitable?*

DR: Getting people through the doors initially. Once they've been through the doors most of them want to come back.

LW: *What's the throughput at the Dungeons at the moment?*

DR: The throughput will be more than 575,000 people this year. We've gone up from 400,000 in the past two or three years, and we expect that figure to rise further.

LW: *What is the history of Kunick's involvement with the London Dungeons?*

DR: We bought London Dungeons in 1983, but It had been running for about eight years before that. The Dungeons were making a profit when we bought it of £200,000.

LW: *And what are the forecasts for this year?*

DR: Well we made about £1.2 million pre-tax profits in the year to September 1989. We will at least equal that this year. I always like to break profit forecasts, I like to pride myself on that. I think it's really bad to do a budget and know you haven't got a cat in hell's chance of achieving it. I used to be involved in Trident Television, running their leisure division, and I never failed to meet my budgets.

LW: *Have you changed the concept of the Dungeons much over the years?*

DR: Oh yes, we've changed it, we've put more animation into the Dungeons.

I really didn't want to be an operator, but I was brought in two years ago last February to sort out financial problems. From September 1987 to September 1988 we were forecast to be making about £580,000, but it looked in February as though we were going to make £520,000, so I came in then to operate the Dungeons. In September we finished up with year profits of just over £1 million, and a year later - in spite of the hot summer and the rail strikes - we still came in with £1.2 million.

LW: *How did you achieve this turnaround?*

DR: I would like to think it is a question of the right promotions and running the place properly. We aren't over-staffed, we watch the staff carefully and we've got a good bunch of people. We've got 26 people, which is low, and our advertising budget is similarly low. We do a lot of promotion ourselves. When I see some of the advertising budgets in the leisure industry, some of them are a waste of money. We watch our advertising very, very carefully.

We have also been successful, in the past couple of years in building up a functions business at the Dungeons to boost revenue.'

Kunick subsequently sold their Dungeon interests to Merlin Entertainment which now runs Dungeons, on very similar lines, in Blackpool, Edinburgh, London, York and Warwick.
As well as the UK they also have dungeons in Germany and The Netherlands. They are opening the first United States Dungeon in 2014.

# CHAPTER 16

## The Nelson Mandela years

*The late Nelson Mandela*

'By 2012, casino and entertainment impresario Don Robinson has met many of the world's great figures.

From presidents to The Beatles there are not many people the 78-year-old has not shaken hands with but he holds the former South African president above them all.

'Maybe of all the people I've met I feel Nelson Mandela to be the most impressive. I think while he is universally revered it's almost impossible to overstate the difficulties he faced and the level of turmoil in South Africa. Without him there would have been a catastrophe.

My two meetings with him came about in South Africa when we were looking to bring a major cruise liner, which was due to be retired and scrapped, down to Durban. Durban was, at that time, critically short of hotel accommodation and we intended redeveloping the vessel as a floating hotel. It made front page news in South Africa and Nelson Mandela heard about it.

We met twice in South Africa and once in London. I always remember shaking his hand. When I made to take my hand away he kept hold of it for some time and asked about the project and said, 'This is the type of project we badly need in South Africa.

Unfortunately, after much further work and investigation the ship and infrastructure proved to be just too large to berth permanently in the port, so the project couldn't proceed but the meetings with Mandela are something I shall always remember.

I was in South Africa and he came to see a cricket match in which the London Stock Exchange team, of which I am life Vice-President, was playing. He was such a lovely man. I went to Robben Island once and for a man to have been locked up for all those years in a place like that and then to come out and preach peace is something from another world.

I have to admit that when I heard he had died I shed a tear. I have met many people in my life but he was the greatest, I have always told people that.

"When, in hundreds of years' time, people sit down to write the history of the times the first words they will write will be 'Nelson Mandela'.'

Nelson Mandela's full name was Rolihlahla Mandela. He was born on 18th July 1918 in Mvezo, Cape Province, South Africa.

He died aged 95, on 5th December 2013 in Johannesburg, South Africa

Nelson Rolihlahla Mandela was a South African anti-apartheid revolutionary, politician, and philanthropist who served as President of South Africa from 1994 to 1999. He was South Africa's first black chief executive, and the first elected in a fully representative democratic election. His government focused on dismantling the legacy of apartheid through tackling institutionalised racism, poverty and inequality, and fostering racial reconciliation. Politically an African nationalist and democratic socialist, he served as President of the African National Congress from 1991 to 1997. Internationally, Mandela was Secretary General of the Non-Aligned Movement from 1998 to 1999.

A Xhosa born to the Thembu royal family, Mandela attended the Fort Hare University and the University of Witwatersrand, where he studied law. Living in Johannesburg, he became involved in anti-colonial politics, joining the ANC and becoming a founding member of its Youth League. After the South African National Party came to power in 1948, he rose to prominence in the ANC's 1952 Defiance Campaign, was appointed superintendent of the organisation's Transvaal chapter and presided over the 1955 Congress of the People. Working as a lawyer, he was repeatedly arrested for seditious activities and, with the ANC leadership, was unsuccessfully prosecuted in the Treason Trial. Influenced by Marxism, he secretly joined the South African Communist Party and sat on its Central Committee. Although initially committed to non-violent protest, in association with the SACP he co-founded the militant Umkhonto we Sizwe (MK) in 1961, leading a sabotage campaign against the apartheid government. In 1962, he was arrested, convicted of conspiracy to overthrow the state, and sentenced to life imprisonment in the Rivonia Trial.

Mandela served over 27 years in prison, initially on Robben Island, and later in Pollsmoor Prison and Victor Verster Prison. An international campaign lobbied for his release.

He was released in 1990, during a time of escalating civil strife. Mandela joined negotiations with President FW de Klerk to abolish apartheid and establish multiracial elections in 1994, in which he led the ANC to victory and became South Africa's first black president. He published his autobiography in 1995. During his tenure in the Government of National Unity he invited several other political parties to join the cabinet. As agreed during the negotiations to end apartheid in South Africa, he promulgated a new constitution. He also created the Truth and Reconciliation Commission to investigate past human rights abuses. While continuing the former government's liberal economic policy, his administration also introduced measures to encourage land reform, combat poverty, and expand healthcare services. Internationally, he acted as mediator between Libya and the United Kingdom in the Pan Am Flight 103 bombing trial, and oversaw military intervention in Lesotho. He declined to run for a second term, and was succeeded by his deputy, Thabo Mbeki. Mandela became an elder statesman, focusing on charitable work through the Nelson Mandela Foundation.

Mandela was a controversial figure for much of his life. Denounced as a communist terrorist by critics, he nevertheless gained international acclaim for his activism, having received more than 250 honours. He is held in deep respect within South Africa, where he is often referred to by his Xhosa clan name, Madiba, or as Tata ('Father'); he is often described as "the father of the nation'.

# CHAPTER 17

## The Charitable years

With tongue somewhat in cheek, I asked Don how much he thought he, his family and his companies had donated to various charities over the years.

Within half an hour he was back on the telephone – 'donations amount to £636,948'.

A week or so later we met and were discussing this chapter and I commented that from my research and from what he had told me I thought the total figure might have been much higher. Don looked at me and said, 'But that figure was for just one company!'

Whilst records will be available from his various company accounts over the years and as, at one time or another he has been a director of at least 24 companies I decided to pass on that one.

Further enquiry revealed that there were also events which had indirectly helped to raise vast sums for particular charities such as the charitable Live-Aid concert in 1985 at Wembley. Don was involved and agreed that the rent charged by Wembley to Live Aid 'was 'very much reduced'.

So I decided to go through the numerous press cuttings I had accumulated to see if I could get a better idea. But charitable giving of course is not just about money; much of it can be in valuable time given to worthwhile charitable organisations. And much can be virtually unquantifiable many years after the event – for instance, providing accommodation or transport to families who have been hit by tragedy. The following emerged. Don was presented with a Variety Club Golden Heart award for presenting 3 minibuses over a period, through his Kunick Company. The buses together cost around £33,000 and went to various beneficiaries – one to Brompton Hall School, near

Scarborough. Don had been a member and official of the Variety Club for many years so his donations to its worthwhile causes over the years are likely to have been much higher.

The National Society for Cancer Relief benefitted with a donation of £250,000 on 9th December 1983 and in 2003 Don & Jean Robinson donated £10,000 towards the building costs of a replacement Hospice then being built at Throxenby Lane, to replace the original hospice at 137 Scalby Road, Scarborough.

The original hospice had been opened by Princess Margaret, Countess of Snowden, on April 29 1985. I had been invited to attend and I met Don when we parked our cars. Jean Robinson had actually been invited to the opening as a guest but couldn't attend so Don told me he had gone in her place. But even in those days security was extremely tight and there was quite a hiatus as Don handed over Jean's invitation and explained she couldn't attend.

He was questioned and a number of phone calls took place to prove he was who he said he was. Eventually the door opened and we all expected Princess Margaret to appear. But in stepped Don, who made his entrance somewhat sheepishly a couple of minutes before Princess Margaret arrived.

In 1998 when Don was expanding his businesses into Bulgaria he and his companies made many donations.

At Don Valley Stadium, Sheffield, in an event covered by Yorkshire TV, he donated wheelchairs, hospital beds and medical equipment to Bulgaria and paid for the transportation of the items. This total donation amounted to US $100,000.

His companies provided air flights and accommodation for 6 British surgeons to visit Bulgaria and also met the costs of 2 Bulgarian surgeons visiting the UK.

US $20,000 sponsorship was provided to the Karim Dom Foundation – a children's' orphanage in Bulgaria.

During Euro 1996 he arranged and paid for the Bulgarian football team to play a friendly game at Wembley against

England and his companies sponsored US $50,000 for hotel accommodation in the UK for the Bulgarian team who were here for Euro 96.

He also paid and arranged for a visit by Bulgarian TV officials and a Bulgarian TV crew to visit the UK and film in London and Yorkshire and visit the Yorkshire TV studios to talk with management and production teams.

A further sponsorship was to enable UK journalists and photographers to visit Bulgaria.

Various Bulgarian students were sponsored to visit and study in the UK and one was assisted in going to Churchill College in Cambridge. He, after graduating, obtained a job in the financial markets in the City of London.

At current exchange rates these dollar donations amount to around £110,000.

A donation of £6,500 went to the 2011 Armed Forces Day to cover costs for The Yorkshire Volunteers Band and The Blades Air display and at least similar amounts were donated in the two succeeding years making another £13,000.

Assistance was given to an event at Scarborough Castle in HM The Queen's Jubilee year; to an event at Peasholm Park in Scarborough; to help 40 Merchant Navy Veterans visit London as their earlier confirmed hotel booking had 'gone astray'; to a local Dance group and to the Littlefoot Trust – a Scarborough based charity which takes disadvantaged children to London once a year. These various events would probably amount to at least another £20,000.

Then Don's company as owner of the Winston Churchill's Britain at War museum in London, donated the business and its assets to a charitable trust. Press releases quoted this donation as being worth £2.5m.

## The Southwark News reported on June 24 2004:

'The past has been saved for the future thanks to the generosity of a Yorkshire businessman.

Churchill's Britain at War in Tooley Street, London Bridge, is one of the most popular visitor attractions on the school curriculum, with thousands of pupils and others pouring through its doors each year.

But a steady increase in expenditure had placed the future of the attraction in jeopardy until Yorkshire businessman Don Robinson gifted the premises and other assets to the value of £2.5m to the Churchill Trust.

Admiral Sir Jeremy Black, chairman of the trustees, said, 'It is an amazing and wonderful gesture. Churchill's Britain at War is now safe for the future and that will mean good news for the many youngsters who come here to get a taste of the wartime life experienced by their grandparents.

It is also excellent news for our staff. We have a wonderful team here and I am delighted that all the hard work they have put in will not be in vain. Mr Robinson's personal gift has helped tremendously with our annual expenditure and has been a deciding fact in our future.'

Churchill's Britain at War recreates wartime London as well as exhibiting, among other things, the nation's favourite entertainers, ration books, food, air raid shelters, newspapers, and even clothing of World War II vintage.'

The various donations and sponsorship we have traced exceed £3m and were obtained from only a small proportion of the many press articles which would have been written over the years. So our gut feeling is that the true total will be nearer double what we have traced – and possibly a much higher multiplier of that figure.

Don and Jean were invited to royal occasions at least a couple of times following his philanthropic work. One invitation was to Highgrove at the invitation of Prince Charles. A dozen people had been invited to walk round the gardens and then have lunch and Don says it was 'a memorable occasion'.

The second was to Buckingham Palace where Don and Jean had been invited to represent the Variety Club of Great Britain. Accompanying them, but not included in the invite was Russell Bradley and his wife Laila. Russell was first Chief executive of Scarborough Borough Council and, sadly, he died in 1913.

The party of four got to London and to their accommodation, and it was obvious that whilst Laila would love to have been invited, to Don and Russell it was 'just another occasion.'

Eventually Don suggested that Laila went in his place and that whilst the ladies were hobnobbing with royalty the men would do their own thing.

In these days of high security it is difficult to see how invitations could be 'swapped' at that late stage but maybe a call was made, or Jean and Laila were very persuasive when they both arrived, but in the event both were admitted, Laila as 'Mr Robinson'.

The ladies had a wonderful evening amongst a party of around 200, especially so when the Duke of Edinburgh approached them and, with a twinkle in his eye, asked, 'What are you ladies doing on your own?'

# CHAPTER 18

# THE FAMILY YEARS

Don Robinson and Jean Margaret Towell met, became friends, courted and fell in love. They married at St Columba's Church in Columbus Ravine, Scarborough, in 1955 when they were both 21 years old. They have both now achieved their 80th birthdays and their Diamond Wedding Anniversary.

Don was born on 27th June 1934 and Jean, also born in June that year is just a few weeks older. The first house they owned was a bungalow in Box Hill, Scarborough, but around 45 years ago when Don's businesses were doing well and both were still in their mid-30s, they decided to design their own dream home overlooking the sea to the North of Scarborough.

It not only overlooked the sea, but in those days the design was somewhat unusual and was described in 'The Journal' of October 2000 as being 'inspired by the clean white lines of Mediterranean architecture and the opulence of American lifestyles.'

The house is effectively upside down – the upper floor lending itself to general living space because of the fantastic views towards Scarborough Castle and the North Sea. The house also has very large windows which were somewhat unusual at the time it was built, but, as Don says, 'There would be no point in building a house in a position like this and having small windows. We wanted to bring the views into the house. Even when the wind is howling outside and the rain is lashing against the windows, we still have extraordinary views of the coastline.'

The extensive main living room with its large picture windows and fabulous views has, over the years been the focal point of lively evenings with some of the most famous names in British show business. These included Mike & Bernie Winters, Les Dawson, Jimmy Tarbuck and Ken Dodd but there were many more.

Downstairs where some of the bedrooms also benefit from sea views, the Robinsons have created their own space. Their private rooms overlook a pristine, crystal clear, circular swimming pool, surrounded by patio furniture and well-scrubbed flagstones.'

Outside, as well as a sizeable car park area, is Don's helipad - originally used when he was a director of Trident TV (Trident owned Yorkshire TV and Tyne Tees TV) and he would be picked up for Board Meetings in Trident TV Chairman James (later Sir then later still Lord] Hanson's helicopter.

This latter period led to the book's cover design where Jean can be seen in the window waving to Don who is being hoisted aboard the helicopter. Don being hoisted aboard is, of course, sheer artistic licence but the idea came from the menu cover of a Christmas Press lunch which Don held in December 1973. This followed Don and a number of friends and colleagues hoodwinking the world's press into an April Fool's day joke. Don's team 'captured' the Loch Ness Monster. The Guinness Book of Records claimed this to be one of the best ever April Fool's Day jokes.

Returning to The Journal article, 'Everything in the Robinsons' home is geared towards relaxation and entertaining. 'We are much more family and socially oriented than design and fashion oriented,' said Jean.
'We don't want the kind of home where people can't feel relaxed.'

The article continues, 'The Robinsons are genuinely warm and hospitable. Jean plies visitors with fresh-brewed coffee and biscuits while Don enthuses about the home, his business and life in general. He's as enigmatic as his long and varied career suggests and he's spent many evenings reminiscing well into the night about the landmarks which have made him a legend in his own lifetime.

This is the man who set up Flamingo Park; launched all night dances in Bridlington; brought Little Richard to East Yorkshire; started Scarborough's Zoo and Marineland, fought in the wrestling ring for 12 years as Dr Death, then promoted wrestling, was President of Scarborough Cricket Club for 2 years, owned Dudley Zoo and Windsor Safari Park, became chairman of Scarborough, then Hull City Football Clubs, and who now has businesses in Bulgaria, where he was one of the first British investors.'

The accomplishments above are just a tiny part of Don Robinson's overall achievements and he treasures and is proud of being a Freeman of Las Vegas, USA; of Scarborough his adopted town, and also of London.

Don and Jean have two sons, Nick and Andrew. Nick has two daughters, Georgia and Claudia who both work in London; Andrew, whose wife Anni is Bulgarian, has a daughter Kristiana and a son James. Both Nick and Andrew look after the family's interests in Bulgaria.

It would be fair to assume that Don and Jean could live anywhere in the world and leave their family home in Scarborough.

'We've thought of moving to London, or Europe, or America. But in the end we've always come to the conclusion that Scarborough is where we want to be,' Don said.

'It's where our friends are. It's what we know. Why move for the sake of moving - when home is where the heart is?'

Now, with both Don and Jean over 80 and with their Diamond Wedding Anniversary approaching; with many of their business interests sold on or being looked after by their sons; they can enjoy their retirement and relax in the home they love.

Except, that personally I feel Don will never retire. His brain is still as sharp as a needle and whilst his memory of things long ago sometimes requires a little nudging and this exasperates him, he still visits his modest office in Scarborough's Westborough twice a week – an office adorned with old theatre bills, wrestling posters and photographs of past ventures and personalities, including a framed, signed photograph from the late Lord Hanson of whom Don says, 'James Hanson as he was when I first got to know him was a brilliant man.'

In his office he meets old clients and friends. He signs letters and cheques which his long serving and seemingly non-flappable Personal Assistant Roseanne Archer has prepared for him.

And still Don talks and thinks about the future.

Reading takes him some time, as these days poor eyesight means he needs to use a magnifying glass, but on my last visit he handed to me a draft advertisement that appears at the end of this chapter.

'What's that?' I asked. 'In my research I've come across nothing mentioning a 'British Empire Leisure Theme Park'.'

'Oh that', said Don somewhat nonchalantly, but with a twinkle in his eye. 'That's the latest venture. It's something new we're working on.' And almost as an aside he says, 'By the way, we are also working on two or three new things in Bulgaria. They will all happen soon.'

Without any doubt, they will.

Officially in retirement, some of the load has been lifted from Don by his two sons, but he still has immense drive and perseverance to get a job finished on time, successfully and profitably.

For over well over 60 years Don Robinson has been, and will remain, one of our country's highest of High Fliers.

***

Lightning Source UK Ltd.
Milton Keynes UK
UKHW010632150322
400092UK00001B/89